Journey On

THROUGH THIS SHADOWED VALLEY

DAPHNE SELF

Journey On
Through This Shadowed Valley

©2020 by Daphne Self
All rights reserved

ISBN: 978-1-62020-732-1
eISBN: 978-1-62020-752-9
Library of Congress Control Number: 2020949259

Cover Design and Page Layout by Frederick Design
Digital Edition by Anna Riebe Raats

Oatman, Jr., Johnson. "Count Your Blessings." 1856-1922. Public Domain.

Unless otherwise marked, Scripture taken from the New King James Version®. Copyright © 1982 by Thomas Nelson. Used by permission. All rights reserved.

Scripture marked NLT taken from the *Holy Bible*, New Living Translation, Copyright © 1996, 2004, 2015 by Tyndale House Foundation. Used by permission of Tyndale House Publishers, Inc., Carol Stream, Illinois 60188. All rights reserved.

Scripture marked NASB taken from the NEW AMERICAN STANDARD BIBLE®, Copyright © 1960, 1962, 1963, 1968, 1971, 1972, 1973, 1975, 1977, 1995 by The Lockman Foundation. Used by permission.

Scripture marked NIV taken from the Holy Bible, New International Version®, NIV® Copyright ©1973, 1978, 1984, 2011 by Biblica, Inc.® Used by permission. All rights reserved worldwide.

Scripture marked KJV taken from the King James Version. Public Domain.

AMBASSADOR INTERNATIONAL
Emerald House
411 University Ridge, Suite B14
Greenville, SC 29601, USA
www.ambassador-international.com

AMBASSADOR BOOKS
The Mount
2 Woodstock Link
Belfast, BT6 8DD, Northern Ireland, UK
www.ambassadormedia.co.uk

The colophon is a trademark of Ambassador, a Christian publishing company.

DEDICATION

FIRST AND FOREMOST, I DEDICATE THIS book to my Lord Jesus Christ. Without Him, this would not be possible, and He sees me through it all.

To Nate, who has been my rock and steady hand: your love and support can never be quantified. You are the epitome of a loving and godly husband.

To my sons, Caleb and Blake: you two have been there through it all; and your support, help, and love see me through even the toughest of days.

To my mom, Betty Sue: you never leave me, are always there for me, and are always trying to understand and help. For all you do, I will be forever grateful. You are the most awesome mom in the world.

To my online friends in Heartwings: it was you who caused this book to be born. With each Scripture you sent my way, you brought me from the brink and helped set me on solid ground.

To my author friends and new friends: we are in this together. Thank you for your love and support!

ENDORSEMENTS

Daphne Self's *Journey On: Through This Shadowed Valley* is an illuminating account of the daily struggles faced by fibromyalgia and chronic pain patients. The author finds consolation in her Christian faith, but this is a must-read for anyone with FMS who feels lost, confused, and alone; or for their family members or friends. Helpful references are included where to seek more information. Fibromyalgia is a genuine disease, which recent evidence is confirming, and this "real and raw" book reveals its devastating effects on the sufferer.

Ronda L. Wells, MD

The blunt honesty that Daphne reveals as she struggles with fibromyalgia provides hope to those who deal with lifelong chronic pain. Her relationship with Jesus during the worst of times shows through our weakness Jesus shows His strength. If we lay our sorrows before Christ He will lift them from our shoulders just as He promised when He said "My yoke is easy and My burden is light" (Matthew 11:30). Daphne's journey gives hope to those who believe they have no hope, and that hope is found in Jesus.

Ann Allen, author of *Out of Darkness*

Journey On: Through This Shadowed Valley by Daphne Self paints a picture of chronic illness. The book's daily descriptions of pain and loss are woven into the author's strong faith, which sees her through the valleys of her disease. The book will help others who have chronic illnesses feel less alone as it educates all to the depth of suffering and daily struggles of those with chronic diseases.

Gail Pallotta, a Reader's Favorite Award Winner and TopShelf 2020 Nominee

CONTENTS

DEDICATION	V
ENDORSEMENTS	VII
PREFACE	1
WHAT IS FIBROMYALGIA?	3
AUTHOR'S AFTERWORD	91
FOODS AND DIET PLANS	93
MIGRAINE DIET	93
TESTIMONIES	97
MELINDA GREEN	98
TONI HIBBERD-JUDKINS	100
LESLIE L. MCKEE	104
CARRIE DEL PIZZO	110
TOM DONNAN	118
RENEE BLARE	126
RESOURCES	129
BOOKS FOR ADDITIONAL READING	131

PREFACE

AS I START THIS JOURNAL, I do it to help me. To help me discover myself, to accept and manage my condition, to carry me, to strengthen me, to encourage me, and to change me.

It's not my words that will do this; it's God's. As I read through Scripture that my sisters-in-Christ have given me, I will journal my thoughts and feelings. I will be raw and honest. I will hold nothing back.

This isn't my struggle alone. There are millions out there who suffer alongside me. I want to show unity and where comfort can be found. There have been many who are seeing me through this. There are many who have opened my eyes to my own selfishness. There have been many who have increased my compassion.

So many lives touch, connect, and intersect. Some for a season; some for a lifetime.

I will be honest about how this journaling frightens me. I close off, shut away, and lock up thoughts and feelings that are unpleasant. But in order to grow, to be able to be what God is wanting me to be, I must confront what I fear.

And I fear pain: physical, emotional, and mental.

I fear loss: loss of self, loss of ability, loss of strength, loss of memory, loss of independence.

I know that many readers do not share the same faith as I, but this isn't about pushing God onto those who don't believe. This book is about showing how I travel through this valley. Because my faith is such an integral part of my life, it is only natural for me to refer to it and to lean upon it. It is my hope that through me, you can find a way to help yourself and to know that you are not alone.

Lord, help me see what You want me to become. Help me through my downfalls. Keep my fears and pride at bay as I do Your will. In Jesus' name, Amen.

WHAT IS FIBROMYALGIA?

FIBROMYALGIA IS MY DIAGNOSIS. IT IS what I will refer to quite often, but with this condition comes a host of others: irritable bowel syndrome, interstitial cystitis, migraines, arthritis—just to name a few.

But what is fibromyalgia?

Fibromyalgia isn't entirely understood, but many doctors and specialists believe it may be caused by a change in the central nervous system in which pain signals that are normally perceived as minor become more intense. In other words, even a gentle hug can be painful. This disorder causes muscle pain and body stiffness. Fatigue is a major symptom for those who have fibromyalgia. And because of the extreme pain, insomnia is another symptom.

Fibromyalgia may make it difficult for someone to work or perform everyday activities, such as walking, laundry, shopping, etc. With this condition, the person can have good days and bad days. They may look fine on the outside; but inside, they are struggling with pain, fatigue, and insomnia. This is why fibromyalgia is referred to as an "invisible disease." And this is a chronic condition. It may come and go but will never go away completely. It is a frustrating and limiting illness.

Living with fibromyalgia means making adjustments. The way of life we once knew may have to change; and many times, our way of life disappears, and a new way is born. Family and friends can help someone with fibromyalgia by following the advice below:

- Ask how that person is doing and really listen to the answer.
- Educate yourself on fibromyalgia. This will help you support your loved one.
- Take an active role in their care. Go to doctor's appointments, take notes, and provide moral support.
- Offer practical help, such as shopping or doing household chores. Offer emotional support by being patient, caring, and loving.
- Set goals together and encourage one another.
- Do things you enjoy to reduce stress. Help your loved one reduce stress by being there for them.

This is just a small list of helpful advice that was gleaned from many sources (which are listed at the end of the book). The best way to learn is to research.

October 27, 2018

PSALM 57:1-3

Be merciful to me, O God, be merciful to me!
For my soul trusts in You;
And in the shadow of Your wings I will make my refuge,
Until these calamities have passed by.
I will cry out to God Most High,
To God who performs all things for me.
He shall send from heaven and save me;
He reproaches the one who would swallow me up. Selah
God shall send forth His mercy and His truth.

WHEN I WAS DIRECTED TO THIS verse by a friend—one who suffers from fibromyalgia, too—I realized how powerful it resonated within me.

Today, of all days, I struggle with pain. As I told one of my fellowship groups, my fingers have electric rods instead of bones, and my body curls up like a frightened armadillo—and not by my choice!

Pain is scary to me. Not because of how it feels. Usually, pain passes with time and healing; but in this instance, I face a pain that is beyond my comprehension. Beyond my control. Beyond my ability to handle. And that is the problem for me. The pain becomes so loud that it takes my focus away from God. My thoughts become a jumble of erratic connections.

When I read Psalm 57, the first line screamed at me: "Be merciful to me, O God, be merciful to me!"

I am screaming this deep inside my mind and soul. *Please, be merciful!*

I feel like a cartoon character melting into a puddle and screaming, "The pain! The pain!" And I realize that I am concentrating on the pain and not on the Lord.

Pain becomes heightened as thoughts activate neurons, and the pain receptors become hypersensitive. The more I concentrate on it, the more the pain messages are sent.

When I look at Psalm 57:1-3, I see more than calling out to God. I see trust. I must trust in Him. He's changing me. He's molding me. I am in the shadow of His wings. Like a great eagle, He lifts me up to soar and tucks me under His wings to protect me. I am His precious creation. And sometimes, creating something requires a little breaking, a little whittling, and a little molding.

God will give me what I need—not what I want, but what I need. And I am starting to discover that what I need is truly what I want.

God will never allow pain and adversity to defeat me. It is a battle; but in the end, it's God's glory that sees me through.

As I write this, the air is cooler; the breeze is cold; and clouds are moving in. But in it all, I see the bright sunshine of God's love and power shining down on me.

These hills and valleys I trek across will wear me down. As I wear down, I am laid bare. God sees me underneath my humanity, underneath my shield, underneath my stubbornness, underneath my pain and sickness.

He tells me that I am wonderfully made, a beautiful creation (Psalm 139:14). I cannot let the world hide me and clothe me in stubbornness, pride, and selfishness. I need to let God clothe me in His light. Let the world see—even if it's only a few people—that despite this pain, my spirit is not broken. God has given me strength.

Be merciful to me, O God! Beneath Your wings, I find refuge. These calamities will pass, and it is Your merciful grace that will reproach them!

October 28, 2018

2 TIMOTHY 4:17

> *But the Lord stood with me and strengthened me, so that the message might be preached fully through me, and that all the Gentiles might hear. Also I was delivered out of the mouth of the lion.*

WHEN I READ THIS PASSAGE, I can't see how it pertains to me until I read the first part and the last part.

"But the Lord stood with me and strengthened me."

I hear it and read it all the time that our strength alone will not be enough; but what most people don't tell me is how to rely upon God for the strength.

I pray. And yet, I'm still weak.

I read the Bible. And yet, fatigue claims me.

I look to the Lord. And yet, my body betrays me.

My bad days claim me. And all around me, I can see only dirty dishes, dirty laundry, dirty floors. I homeschool, and I haven't been able to update and record grades in over a week. I work as a freelance editor, and my projects are overdue. My pets have fleas. My pantry is empty. And bills need to be paid.

The more I try to do, the worse the situation becomes because I cannot complete one job before moving to the next.

One task deflates my energy. As I struggle to overcome the fatigue induced by chores, everything else multiplies like rabbits on caffeine.

This is where I learn.

As part of my treatment, I attended a group therapy called cognitive behavior therapy. It's intimidating to be around strangers in front of psychologists, but this wasn't a typical group session. The main purpose was to rewire my thought patterns.

Fibromyalgia has stolen from me.

It is here to stay.

I'm not the same as I was before.

In order to learn how to accept and deal with this condition, I had to learn to think differently.

I may not be able to do all I used to do. But I can do some things.

My strength wanes quickly, so I do things in spurts. Dishes? One-pot meals. Fewer dirty pots. Since I love Food Network, I've learned about mise en place ("putting in place"), which means that I pre-cut, pre-slice, pre-measure.

After grocery shopping (sometimes online), I chop celery and carrots and store them in storage containers. Sometimes, I buy pre-cut vegetables.

I also mix spices for dishes. In one bottle is the mixture for cinnamon toast and other cinnamon-y desserts. One container holds an Italian herb mix, while another has the pizza herb mix.

Doing these things cuts down on my movements, which helps preserve my energy.

Above all, I'm not too prideful to ask for help.

Dirty laundry? My son has learned how to do the laundry. He takes care of it; he just won't touch certain articles of mine and his dad's clothing—i.e. underwear. Sometimes, clean clothes become a mountain in which I have to navigate to find a particular shirt. But hey, they're clean!

Dirty floors? Sometimes, they are ignored; but at least once a week, my son vacuums; my husband sweeps; and I mop. I found mopping taxes me less.

Homeschool records and editing jobs have become victims of a schedule. I've always been allergic to rigid schedules; but if I don't devise a way to handle these two important tasks, then I will either overextend myself or become backlogged.

I chose Sundays and Mondays for homeschooling tasks. My son is old enough to do his lessons with very little guidance from me. Every day, I allow three hours for editing, each in one-hour stretches. Once three hours are met, I stop.

I'm usually tired by then, so I rest and go on to things that relax me and let me recoup. Usually this involves reading, playing video games, writing, solving Sudoku, or sleeping.

The point is that I have become weak. I may do things, but I require help. And even when chores overwhelm me, I know that in the grand scheme of things, they don't matter.

God provides me with the strength I need for that day. If I can't do it, then I take my cue—He wants me to rest.

Fibromyalgia is like a hungry lion. It tries to devour me. Its teeth rip and pull at me, tearing away at me; yet God delivers me from its jaws and sets me onto solid ground. The lion isn't defeated, but I'm away from its mouth and able to find a new life.

Maybe that's what it's all about.

God stripped away my old life, even the old life after my salvation. He's given me a new life. I am still adjusting to it; but despite the pain and fatigue, somehow, I will discover that it will be all for God's glory.

Now I understand the passage.

Come what may, God is there right beside me, giving me His strength to journey on.

November 3, 2018

PHILIPPIANS 4:13

I can do all things through Christ who strengthens me.

HOW MANY TIMES HAVE I READ that Scripture? How many times have I heard it? Countless times. And each time, it conveys a different meaning, a different truth.

Today was a bad day. And by bad, I mean really bad. I woke up in pain—excruciating pain—with the inability to walk well. No longer did it feel as though I was walking on a left prosthetic leg, but it only dragged a few inches at a time. My body felt racked with waves and battering rams of pain assaulting me.

And this was a day I could not afford to stay home.

My mom was finally in Iowa. After six years of prayer, she sold her house and was now calling Iowa home. We needed to help my brother and her unload her things.

So after struggling to rise and dress, to walk down the flight of stairs and to the car, and then eventually to cross the street to my brother's condo, I was exhausted. I could only shuffle inch by inch with my husband's help, much to my family's irritation. They finally saw the extent of my condition, my disease, my affliction. I explained that I needed time to move. It took longer for my brain's messages to reach my legs, and then it took a while for my legs to respond.

But you know what's wonderful about families?

No matter how strong tempers flare and how loud yells can get, they eventually fade away, and everyone is back to joking and laughing.

I may have been in pain, but I took advantage of my brother's easy chair (oh, so comfy!), and I kept my four-year-old nephew occupied and out from underfoot. Blocks, Legos, and dinosaurs kept my mind off my pain.

Hours later, with Mom's things unpacked, I had to return home. One symptom that I was hoping would never happen happened, and I needed to change.

Mom understood.

So, home I went. I messaged her and told her I would be back for my framed picture; it was time I took my medicine.

I mean, how do the very tips of my fingers hurt like that? I couldn't hold a pen. I couldn't type. I couldn't put on socks. There were places on me that I never knew existed!

Soon, though, I slept. The medicine worked quickly, and I fell into a deep and quiet void. My only thought was, *Please, give me strength!*

I woke up. Chatted with my mother and sister-in-law. Tried to do some work but ended up watching The Food Network. It was medicine time again. And again, I fell into a dreamless void. No thought this time as I drifted away.

When I awoke, the pain refused to budge.

It was the weather. It was the stress. It was just one of those days. All I knew was that I finally understood what a flare-up was.

How would I make it through? So much pain from teeth to fingertips to knees to toes . . .

There were people praying for me. That I knew. I knew I would make it through. So, I huddled under my blanket and nestled against my husband as he played a video game. There I stayed until it was time for bed.

After my husband helped me dress and climb into bed, I knew that I still had the strength to see this through. There was a reason for this suffering, and I would ride it through because this was only a small moment in time.

As I drifted to sleep, my mind played one refrain over and over. In my head, I sang one line of a song by Unspoken: "Just Give Me Jesus."

And that night I dreamed.

I dreamed a doctor was examining my leg. I told him it didn't concern me half as much as my spine. He had me lie back and roll toward him. He pressed, pushed, and prodded around the bad area of my spine. It was painful, but I trusted him. For a long time, this happened. The more he pressed, the worse it hurt—but the more my strength grew. His fingers slid into my back, touching the worst part of my spine and spinal cord and around it. Pops and twangs could be heard and felt.

Then it all faded, and I gradually woke up.

I could move my leg.

The excruciating pain had receded. The stiffness and tightness had nearly vanished. The pain that I felt was more of an annoyance. Was I better? Definitely! Was I healed? No. Not yet.

No more cold, burning pain. No more screaming-in-my-head pain.

God sent an angel. Prayers were answered. I asked for Jesus, and Jesus sent me help. He sent me strength.

Was it just a dream? Maybe. Was it the only way my mind was able to perceive what was happening? Probably. But it doesn't matter. To me,

I believe that I was given relief and strength to keep going. "I can do all things through Christ," right?

But what if it didn't always mean doing something physically? What if it meant that through Christ, Who gives me strength, I am able to reach out and cling to that lovely cross? Maybe it means that through Christ, I am given the strength to keep turning to Him in prayer, even when the prayer on my lips is the words, "Just give me Jesus."

Maybe through my spiritual strength, I will eventually gain my physical strength. I can see the promise in that Scripture: "I can do all things through Christ who strengthens me."

November 5, 2018

ZECHARIAH 10:12

> "*So I will strengthen them in the LORD,*
> *And they shall walk up and down in His name,*"
> *Says the LORD.*

I'VE BEEN TIRED. I'VE BEEN WEAK. I may be able to walk better since my dream, but I battle weakness and fatigue.

For a while, I've been wanting to write. I compose the words in my head; but by the time I apply pen to paper, they fade away.

My feelings of failure about homeschooling fade away.

My irritation at not being able to clean my house fades away.

All other negative thoughts fade away because I read the verse from Zechariah.

My sister has been sending me encouraging messages. I receive messages from friends and fellow authors, asking me how I'm doing, telling me a joke or encouraging story, or just dropping a note to say hi.

Strength comes in a variety of forms, I realized. God sends people into my life. Some for a season and some for a lifetime. These are all my brothers and sisters in Christ; some just don't know it yet!

Today, I received my trigger point injections. These allow me to walk. Numerous shots are injected around my spine and hips to reduce the inflammation and pain. I'm still on two medications, each designed to control the nerve pain. And maybe, just maybe, my insurance will approve a new medication to help me with fibromyalgia. Today, I was officially diagnosed with fibromyalgia. We still have to wait before I can have another MRI. So, it is all about controlling my symptoms.

That's the problem with chronic pain. It steals so much from a person. With me, it was hiking. I can barely walk, can't work, and can barely stand. I had to relearn who I am.

My disease doesn't define me.

My weakness doesn't define me.

My lack of mobility doesn't define me.

My cognitive problems don't define me.

My pain doesn't define me.

Each of these may slow me down, may interfere with my everyday activities, may hamper my style—but they can't defeat me.

No one said that my walk "up and down" had to be at a run. No one said I had to jog or climb many steps. No one said that my walk couldn't be little steps or toddler-style climbs.

No one said I had to run a marathon or even walk a walk-a-thon.

My "walk up and down in His name" is my journey.

As I write this, I realize I'm not the same person I was a month ago or even a year ago. Fibromyalgia has changed me. It changed me physically. It changed me emotionally. It changed me mentally. It changed me spiritually.

Physically, I'm weaker. Now instead of being headstrong and independent, I'm dependent on my family and mainly on my husband. I do not try to do it all on my own. There's no need in that. I accept the help, gladly.

Emotionally, I'm content. I no longer bemoan my loss or question why. I no longer allow depression or stress to best me. It is still a battle, but I have the armor and weapons to defeat those emotions that want to drag me down into the pit.

Mentally, I have changed. I've accepted the fact that I forget things. I am at peace that I struggle at times to remember the simplest of words. I know that I can keep my brain strong through words games—such as crosswords or Scrabble—or number games, such as Sudoku. I read and write. What I forget, I write down to remind me. I also remind myself that even though my IQ is up there, Einstein (who was a total genius!) even forgot his own address, and his wife had to come find him. So for us who forget, we are keeping good company.

Spiritually, I have strengthened. As my body weakens, my spirit strengthens.

My walk with the Lord won't always be in a garden or in the quiet of dawn or dusk. My walk is in how I turn to Him. It is how I rely on Him. It is how I love Him. It is how I think of Him.

Up and down—be it emotionally, mentally, or physically—I travel those hills and valleys of life with the Lord at my side—or, at times, in His arms.

Each time I turn to Jesus, I'm given the right amount of strength needed for that particular time. Even as pain stabs through my feet and hands, even as stiffness claims my muscles, I still feel strengthened by the Lord. Trials and tribulations, hills and valleys, ups and downs—I can travel these because I am strong. Even in my weakness, I am strong.

November 8, 2018

ROMANS 5:2

> [Lord Jesus Christ] through whom also we have access by faith into this grace in which we stand, and rejoice in the hope of the glory of God.

ANYONE WHO SUFFERS FROM ANY TYPE of chronic pain knows that at times, hope is all we have. It reminds me of the song by For King & Country, "Hope Is What We Crave." Although, I know that the verse above is usually taught to mean that at the Lord's return, we will see His glory fully revealed, see Him as He truly is, and share in His glory. Despite that long-standing meaning, I see it as something more.

Through my faith in His grace which was given to me, I can rejoice and sing in the hope I am also given. God's unconditional love gives me the freedom to obey Him and live my life for Him.

Maybe that is the reason for my pain. This has slowed me, kept me from pursuing self-generated and self-glorifying endeavors. It was never intentional, but I would try to gain recognition or some sort of praise. I fell into that trap of believing that unless I receive those social media "likes" and "shares," I was unsuccessful—I was nothing.

I had taken my eyes off Jesus.

I didn't want to rejoice in the hope of seeing the glory of God. At the time, I wanted to rejoice in the glory of people's praise.

Now that I've been forced to slow down, forced to ask for help, and forced to give up my independence, I have learned that my worth lives in Jesus Christ.

Pain racks my body, and I cry out to Jesus.

Fatigue claims my strength, and I cling to Jesus.

Relief bolsters my strength, and I praise Jesus.

Blessings are sent my way, and I glorify Jesus.

Good or bad, my days revolve around Jesus.

It doesn't mean my every waking minute is spent in prayer or in thought of only my Lord; but He's there in the back of my mind as I work on editing jobs, on homeschooling lessons, through daily tasks, and through doctor appointments. He's never far from me.

I have to adhere to that truth. If not, I would fall apart. I would fall into despair. I would come apart and drown. I would give up.

It reminds me of the 1985 movie adaptation of *Anne of Green Gables*. Anne laments and asks Marilla if she could ever imagine herself in the depths of despair. Marilla answers, "No, I cannot. To despair is to turn your back on God."[1] When I watched the movie, that scene stuck with me and still does today. Why should I despair? I have no reason.

When bad days happen or when I can't do what I think or believe I should be able to do, I should always turn to God. He wants me to talk to Him. Cry out to Him. Smile with Him. Enjoy the silence with Him. In all I do, it should be with Jesus always with me.

---

[1] Colleen Dewhurst, *Anne of Green Gables*, TV-miniseries, Kevin Sullivan, Canada: Canadian Broadcasting Corporation, 1985.

My faith and His glory give me access to Him. My hope is in His glory. And His glory is always going to be there throughout my days here on Earth and then forevermore in Heaven with Him. What more could I ask for?

November 9, 2018

ISAIAH 57:10

> *You are wearied in the length of your way;*
> *Yet you did not say, "There is no hope."*
> *You have found the life of your hand;*
> *Therefore you were not grieved.*

I READ THIS PASSAGE, AND AT first, I couldn't glean anything from it. Here, the Prophet Isaiah is speaking to Israel about her idolatry. Then it dawned on me. Idolatry doesn't only mean having an idol or statue that I pray to; it doesn't only mean worshiping a false god.

No. Idolatry happens whenever I put something above God. If I focus on my pain, I put it above God. If I trust only in my doctors and medication, I put them above God. If I listen only to my husband, then I put him above God. If I bask in my good day, then I am elevating it above God.

I can focus on my pain to help myself make it through the day, but I cannot let it become the foremost thought. If I share it with Jesus, then my burden is lightened.

I can trust my doctors and hope that the medications prescribed will help, but I cannot let them become the ones I trust the most. If I trust only in Jesus, then His promises to me will come to fruition.

I can listen to my husband and love him, but I cannot raise him above God. When I keep Christ in my marriage, then my marriage stays strong, and we are blessed.

I can bask in joy when my good days come, but I cannot let my happiness of a good day be greater than my happiness in the Lord. Honestly, nothing can compare to the happiness I find in Jesus. When I smile, Christ smiles.

I've realized that when I put Christ first, He brings me help. When I hurt, a friend might come along with a sweet, encouraging word. My family share jokes to make me smile or send a message from across the miles to ask how I'm doing. I receive a hug from my son and husband. I am given the perfect cup of coffee by my son. I'm held when I least expect it. Each of these are small things, yet they have huge impacts upon me. They turn my bad day into a day of hope.

Even if I couldn't pick up a pen, I could watch television with my family. Even if I couldn't sit up for long, I could listen to my kid regale me with humorous stories concerning his work or a game he played.

Maybe that is what the sentence is about: I did not say, "There is no hope." There is always hope. It just may never appear the way I believed it should have appeared.

God gave me hope. When the world tried to rip it away and when my body tried to replace it with endless pain, I looked beyond the flimsy barriers and saw God.

He said, "A little bit longer."

So what if I can't hike or climb stairs? So what if every day is an unknown? So what if fatigue, pain, and a host of other problems want to camp out in my life? So what if I am wearied beyond measure?

When Jesus slipped His hand into mine and lifted me up, I found life and was no longer grieved by my afflictions.

This has taught me compassion. Who else out there hurts, but does not know Jesus? He's not a magical Band-aid, but He does make life bearable. I put away all that pulls me away from Him. I look away from those idols that want to claim my heart. I look to Jesus, knowing that through Him, I have hope and—even better—I have life.

November 12, 2018

ROMANS 15:13
Now may the God of hope fill you with all joy and peace in believing, that you may abound in hope by the power of the Holy Spirit.

MY STUDY BIBLE SAYS THIS ABOUT the verse: "The Holy Spirit imparts not only spiritual gifts to the believer, but also joy and peace and hope." But I see it as much more. When there is joy and peace, there is always hope through our belief in Christ. And it's that hope that I cling to throughout my days. Without it, I wouldn't survive.

A few days ago, I visited my mom at my brother's house (the reason for the gap in my entries). My sister-in-law was sick and at home. My nephew ran to the door when he saw us. He doted on our attention; and when he finally lay down for his nap, we had to leave. We had one more errand to run, and my husband had to get ready for work.

We had stopped by to visit because Blake had class at his homeschool extension. After arriving home, Gabe woke up and cried for me. "His Dass" was gone. So after he left work, my brother swung by and picked up Blake and me.

I spent at least four hours there that night. Time was spent playing with Gabe; up and down the stairs we went. I showed him practical jokes to play on his parents and his mammaw with bubble wrap. Then he wanted me to bathe him. And up and down the stairs some more.

It was a great visit; but I paid for it dearly. Was it worth it? Yes. Although I knew the pain that would follow from overexertion, it was unthinkable to not go and see my nephew. He was more important than a no.

In cognitive behavior therapy, we were taught that it was okay to tell people no because our well-being was more important than their wants. That is true sometimes, but this wasn't one of those times.

When I visited my nephew, it alleviated some of my pain. His unconditional love for me pushed all my problems to the side. His smile, hugs, and laughter gave me hope to survive another day.

And the pain the next day? It was there, but not in such a degree that it had been before. It was tolerable, manageable.

What did I learn from this? Sacrifice. Unconditional, loving sacrifice.

Being with family is fun, not relaxing. Joy can be found, and it abounds whenever we are together. We will joke, insult, and rib each other, but it's done in love and with laughter. And there's peace to be found with joy. Those few hours gave me peace from pain. It gave me joy that drowned the encroaching depression.

God knows what I need, especially in my lowest times. He gave me my family and spoke through my four-year-old nephew.

I pray for those who do not have family. I pray that they find one because family does not have to be blood. It is the love that binds people together that makes them family.

And for those who have family—no matter how estranged—I pray that they can find the peace and joy with them as I have with mine. Joy and peace bring me love, which erases my pain.

November 13, 2018

2 CORINTHIANS 12:9

And He said to me, "My grace is sufficient for you, for My strength is made perfect in weakness." Therefore most gladly I will rather boast in my infirmities, that the power of Christ may rest upon me.

"FOR WHEN I AM WEAK, THEN I am strong." I love this portion from the last part of verse ten in 2 Corinthians.

"For when I am weak"—yes, that is me today.

"Then I am strong"—yes, only through Christ.

I was given a print-out about fibromyalgia. I'm still learning about this condition, disease—whatever they want to call it. Here's what fibromyalgia can cause:

Muscle Pain	Numbness/tingling
Irritable bowel syndrome	Dizziness
Fatigue/weakness	Insomnia
Thinking and remembering problems	Depression
	Constipation
Muscle weakness	Nausea
Headache	
	Nervousness
Pain/cramps in abdomen	

Chest pain	Hives/welts
Loss of appetite	Ringing in ears
Rash	Vomiting
Sun sensitivity	Heartburn
Hearing difficulties	Oral ulcers
Easy bruising	Loss/change in taste
Blurred vision	Seizures
Fever	Dry eyes
Diarrhea	Shortness of breath
Dry mouth	Hair loss
Itching	Frequent urination
Wheezing	Painful urination
Raynaud's Syndrome	Bladder spasms

I had to mark which symptoms applied to me. This was tallied to determine my Symptom Severity Score.

The score can change from week to week. When my nerves go haywire, I'll have more symptoms. I mean, the nervous system is the body's information highway, and mine just ran amok. No one knows the reason why. My body broke slightly. My inner workings developed a fracture, and I couldn't repair it. Somehow, information from the brain either went to the wrong place or flooded too many systems with too many messages.

That's the only way I can explain what's happening in my body. And all this misfiring causes the dreaded "fibro fog," causes my hands to struggle to write or type, causes my feet to stumble and barely move, causes my body to falter and become as weak as a flappy baby turtle.

And when I am at my lowest, that is when I feel Christ at His strongest. My human way, flawed and narcissistic, no longer impedes me. I have to rely on Someone besides myself; and even though I have my husband and son here with me, I know they can only do so much. It is Christ Who sees me through.

He see my depression when I hide it from others.

He sees my pain when I downplay it for their sake.

He sees my spirit when I doubt myself and what I do.

He see every hidden aspect of me.

I falter. I fall. I fumble.

He's there to lift me and love me.

His strength provides for me.

I can make it one more day. I have enough strength for that.

November 14, 2018

1 PETER 5:9

Resist him, steadfast in the faith, knowing that the same sufferings are experienced by your brotherhood in the world.

I KNOW THIS PASSAGE SPEAKS ABOUT resisting the devil and his cunning ways, but I see more in it. When I am at my weakest, it's so easy to fall into sin.

I'm irritable. I snap at my husband and son. I cannot honor my husband if I'm willing to snap at him and cause dissension.

I'm in pain. I lash out or ignore those who want to help.

I'm depressed. I think only of myself and ignore all around me.

I must resist all of this. I must. If I stay true to my faith, I can overcome these harmful and sinful feelings. I call them sinful because they can lead to sin.

Irritability, pain, and depression are normal reactions to a disease or condition. But if I allow it to take over my life, I have then set something higher than Christ—and that's idolatry.

I'm not alone in this kind of fight. The Scripture means those who are persecuted for Christ, but it can also mean those who suffer an illness and fight the ongoing battles it causes.

Knowing that others suffer as I do—if not more so—doesn't bring me comfort. It gives me strength knowing that I have a support group who understands. It gives me empathy for those who suffer far greater than me. It gives me joy to see them overcome a difficulty—no matter how small.

Although my connection with others who suffer with chronic pain is limited, I do cherish the few friends that I have. They have become my go-to when I need to vent or when I need to understand.

Living like this is a constant learning environment. Even when it takes a long time to remember a simple word, I've learned to play a back-up game.

For instance, I forgot the word "environment." To remember, I thought to myself, "What was my last word written? What was I holding? What was I looking at? What was the previous word before that? What was my first half of the sentence?"

Boom! I remembered!

It doesn't always work, and sometimes I resort to "whatchamacallit" or "do-hickey." Hey, whatever works, right?

I do laugh at myself. Because it can be funny at times. And life can't always be so serious.

I adapt. I find ways to do what is needed. I accept. I am grateful for help. I learn. I listen to those with experience. I hope. I cling to the belief that no matter what, all will end well, and things will turn out for the best.

If I hurt, I enjoy my fluffy pillow.

If I'm tired, I enjoy my nap.

If I can't walk, I enjoy my time with my family.

If I can't write, I enjoy a good movie or show.

If I can't cook, I enjoy take-out because that's better than my husband or son burning down the apartment!

So tonight, I hurt, but I can write. It takes me longer to remember some words, but I can do it. I may look back on this and wonder what in the world I was rambling about; but writing keeps my mind active, and reading Scripture keeps my faith strong.

November 20, 2018

---

2 CORINTHIANS 1:7
And our hope for you is steadfast, because we know that as you are partakers of the sufferings, so also you will partake of the consolation.

WHAT IS CONSOLATION? COMFORT GIVEN TO a person after a loss or disappointment? Sounds like a parent to me.

I remember so well all the times my parents consoled me—whether the disappointment was great or small. It didn't matter because their love for me was unconditional, and they didn't want to see their daughter hurting.

Years ago, when my sons' father died, my father came to me. I sat, still in shock, in that great, red easy chair of ours. My dad stood by the chair, placed his hand on my head, and said only two words: "Oh, Lulu."

One touch on my head offered more comfort to me than a thousand words.

Today, I no longer have my father with me. I no longer hear him call me Lulu. But I have a Heavenly Father Who provides all the consolation I need.

I cling to my hope. It seems I suffer days at a time. Pain will rack my body. Fatigue claims me as its prisoner. Through the days of suffering, even when reading is lost to me, I know it won't last long. After it comes and goes, I find that the Lord bore me through it all.

I can write in this journal how much I praise Him, how much I love Him, how much I look to Him; but all this is evident in my life.

I find journaling hard. Most days, I want to rail against the unfairness of it all. Some days, I want to express how I've come to accept it all. Then there are the true days: I have no idea what I feel. I can only go about my day and do the best I can. Isn't that all we are required to do? Do only our best.

My best is taking the days I can move freely (a generalized term) and do what I can. On the days where I can't, then I rest; I take it easy and don't fight against the pain, fatigue, "fog," and myriad symptoms that come with all this.

There is one common factor, though. I keep studying and learning. For instance, I found an article at a website called HealthRising. After reading, I determined that there is a definite correlation between migraines and fibromyalgia. As I stated to a friend, I can imagine fibromyalgia on one end and CRP (Complex Regional Pain) on the other with tendrils connecting them. The tendrils are symptoms related to both, and in the middle of the spectrum line are migraines, asthma, and interstitial cystitis (along with irritable bowel syndrome). I have all three of those, and I'm at the fibro end.

This is how I see it:

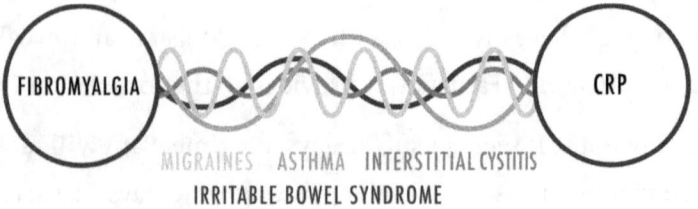

The thing is, I can't stop learning. I have learned that the protein, glutamate, in our body latches onto the inflammation to repair our bodies. Monosodium glutamate is a spice that triggers migraines, and now it makes sense. My body is already hypersensitive. Add more than what I need, and my body goes wonky. It pays to learn as much as I can.

I will suffer. And I receive consolation not only in knowing that my God is near, but also that He gave me the ability to learn. And I am learning what I can do to make my life a little more bearable under these chronic conditions.

November 21, 2018

2 THESSALONIANS 2:16-17
> *Now may our Lord Jesus Christ Himself, and our God and Father, who has loved us and given us everlasting consolation and good hope by grace, comfort your hearts and establish you in every good word and work.*

AFTER STUDYING THESE VERSES AND READING the sidebars and footnotes in my study Bible, I have learned that in the midst of suffering, it is imperative that my devotion to Jesus is strong, that my devotion should continue to grow, and that it should be firmly rooted in the love of God.

I should seek to know God.

I should pursue an ever-deepening relationship with Jesus.

To stand, I should kneel and receive love, eternal comfort, and hope by grace from Jesus Christ.

That is a lot to digest!

When I'm weak, I'm strong—sounds like an oxymoron, but I know in my heart that it's the truth.

I can let weakness destroy me. It would be so easy to give up, but I also know that being weak causes me to look outside myself and see others, the world, and the hope in life.

It's not easy—that's for sure!

Yesterday zapped my strength. I wasn't able to edit, write, nor cook. And that spurred me to research recipes and cooking tips for fibromyalgia sufferers. I found out that a crockpot just may be my best friend. I know some people buy ready-made meals or canned soups, but I'm not able to eat those foods because of the ingredients. So, I've come up with different ways.

I buy frozen veggies. They are already chopped, diced, and cut. I buy pre-cut vegetables. Sometimes, on my good days, I buy onions, chop them, and store or freeze them for later use. At my local grocery store, they are called "shortcuts," and I'm thankful for them.

I spend my good days prepping for the bad days, which usually outnumber the good. So, during my research the other night, I found six crockpot recipes. I'll try them out soon. Even though I'm supposed to increase my protein portions to encourage weight loss, I have to be realistic and know that I can do only so much. But there is a work-around for that, too! I add more meat to the dish.

While prepping the food will help my body, I also use my good days, and even my semi-good days, to record my thoughts. All my distractions are filtered through, and I'm left better able to immerse myself in His Word and to learn to fully rely on Him.

November 22, 2018

PSALM 77:2

> *In the day of my trouble I sought the Lord;*
>
> *My hand was stretched out in the night without ceasing;*
>
> *My soul refused to be comforted.*

GIVE ME BACK MY DIME!

Some people who suffer from a chronic condition where one of the symptoms is extreme fatigue are told about how to reserve energy by thinking of them as spoons. I have no idea what they are talking about, but I did have a physical therapist explain it to me in the form of a dime.

I'm given a dime for the day. The extent or exertion of my activity will determine how much it will cost me.

If I do one load of laundry, then that's one penny. If I do three loads (which also includes the folding and putting away), then that's six pennies.

If I cook a meal, I pay two pennies.

If I shop, I use my dime and borrow against the next day. I had a social media status that read:

10¢ + Walmart = -10¢

I ended up using up that day's energy, as well as the next two days' worth. So, I learned to shop in short spurts. Don't walk the whole store or the whole mall, and definitely don't do both. Or I will find myself demanding that my dime be given back.

When the days come that I'm so tired, so exhausted that even holding a pen or putting on socks is a chore, I find myself not able to be comforted. With fatigue comes pain, and with pain comes fatigue. It's a vicious cycle where I can only cry out to God, over and over. Sometimes, He answers quickly; other times, He is silent, and I continue reaching out to Him.

I will say one thing—it's not easy!

And since today was Thanksgiving, I'm thankful that I was able to be with family. I was thankful that I wasn't given any flak when I had to take my medicine and then lie down on my mom's bed when the medication caused sleepiness.

I was teased about having an emotional support pet. My family didn't understand, or they didn't want to understand, how having a pet like my Chartreux cat, Blue Belle, helps me relax when my bad days happen. Pets intuitively know when we need comfort. Blue Belle will lie beside me or on top of me and stay with me as I sleep or rest. I can pet her. I can listen to her purrs. Or I can relax under her happy-paw kneading.

Having her reduces my stress, which in turn helps reduce my pain. There's an actual chemical reaction that happens inside the body when faced with a stressor, and pain is a major stressor!

Families can be stressors, too. Later on that night, I was teased unmercifully. Thankfully, it was toward the end of the night, and soon, we were preparing to go home. Talking to family is one of the hardest things to do. Do I tell them how much they hurt me?

No. I'll forgive them and move on. But it will limit what I share with them.

For people with chronic conditions, we need support. And support from family is the most cherished of all. Unfortunately, the majority of us don't receive that. And that becomes another stressor.

What I think is even sadder is that a great many who suffer and have no support are also those who don't believe in Jesus or never accepted Him.

Jesus isn't a magical pill that will immediately heal, but He is the One Who offers the comfort that is needed. So, no matter how many times I stretch out my hand, I know He is there holding me. He will never abandon me.

November 23, 2018

PSALM 6:4

> *Return, O LORD, deliver me!*
> *Oh, save me for Your mercies' sake!*

ON PAGE 708, MY STUDY BIBLE says this about the verse: "Sickness is not always a consequence of sin, yet when it is, the pain can be instrumental in bringing the sinner face-to-face with God." I read that, and I say, "Ain't that the truth!"

Pain has a tendency to make me reevaluate. Pain also has a downside: depression. We chronic sufferers know this battle all too well.

Fortunately—or should I say blessedly?—I have not had to endure depression at such a degree that it would call for intervention. But I do struggle with it. My mind will replay words said to me, and I start to spiral downward. I'll start remembering every little detail and then start feeling every little pain.

That causes my body to delve deeper into depression. Once again, there is a chemical reaction within my body which causes the feelings to become heightened. By calling out to God, I can try to refocus my mind. Away from darkness and into light. It's not easy.

Like tonight. I can feel the sadness creeping upon me. Distractions aren't working. Music isn't working. Journaling isn't working. Reading the Bible isn't working.

I know some people would tell me to immerse myself into His Word, and that will help. But not always!

Sometimes, I need to let the depression consume like a dark fire. Then I can rise from it and start anew. It's okay, I tell myself, to cry for no reason. My body needs an outlet.

Let the pain in my feet and toes, my legs and arms, my chest and inside my whole body flow into my eyes and escape as tears. That's how I imagine it.

Even King David cried out to the Lord. It wasn't shouting or yelling loudly. It wasn't a hoarse speech. No, he cried. He shed tears.

Tears are a release. God created tears to wash grief and pain away. So, by allowing myself to cry, I'm allowing my body to cleanse itself of pent-up stress.

There are times when tears won't come. And that is okay, too. I can still cry out and ask for His mercy.

And tonight, it comes in the form of sleep. As my body relaxes, I can find myself drifting away. I will pause and then restart with my writing. Little by little, the pain eases.

Focusing on God isn't always about reading the Bible or memorizing a verse. I can focus on Him by knowing He's always with me. He's holding me because He heard me.

And no matter how jumbled my thoughts may be, He's there seeing me through it all.

P.S. I slow-cooked stroganoff the other night. Noodles do not do well in a crockpot, unless I'm willing to stay on top of it. So, beef stroganoff is a no-go as a fibro one-dish crockpot dinner for me.

November 24, 2018

PSALM 62:5-6

> *My soul, wait silently for God alone,*
> *For my expectation is from Him.*
> *He only is my rock and my salvation;*
> *He is my defense;*
> *I shall not be moved.*

IT'S FUNNY HOW WHEN I'M DOWN, my mind has a tendency to fall back in time. I will relive past hurts and failures, past joys, and long-forgotten dreams.

It doesn't last long, but I'm left with a cold void. And another tendency to quote Shakespeare: "Now is the winter of our discontent."[2]

When I read Richard III (which I haven't done in a long time!), I know that the rest of the soliloquy is stating that the long winter of their troubled history has been transformed into summer by King Edward. But when I take that line by itself, it means more to me: my unhappiness is like winter—cold and gloomy.

Chronic pain, whether by fibromyalgia or migraines, pushes me into a sea of unhappiness, of discontent. I know it's only natural. I mean, I'm only a mere human. I can either sink and drown, tread and remain, or

---

2 (Richard III. 1.1.1)

swim and live. I prefer to swim, albeit slowly and painfully. And I question myself, "How do I turn my winter into summer?"

Well, I honestly love winter. Where I live, I am assured of snow, where it glistens in the sun. The air is purer, and the quiet is more pronounced. But I can tire of winter. Just as I can tire of remaining in a state of depression.

To bring about my summer, my happiness, I search for small things. A hug. A song. A book. A little shopping for gifts (even if it's window shopping). A cuddle with a pet. A view from my window. A game. Being mesmerized by glittery objects.

Then there is the ultimate way to bring about my summer: I read the Psalms. My favorite is Psalm 24: "The earth is the LORD's, and all its fullness, The world and those who dwell therein. For He has founded it upon the seas, And established it upon the waters (vs. 1-2).

It became my favorite when I was a teen. Others learned Psalm 23, but I was drawn to the image of the earth and all upon it belonging to the LORD. The whole expanse—and we are His.

So when my winter of discontent arrives, I know that I am His. He's my Rock, and my Salvation. He turns my winter into summer.

Sometimes, though, I must remain in winter and learn to find beauty in it. Like tonight, the feeling of loneliness and ultimate sadness claimed me. But I used social media to talk with some friends. I texted with my husband while he was at work. I bought a few Christmas presents. Some presents were gifts that also helped a charity. I bought a fellow author's book (*Beast of Stratton* by Renee Blare). I watched a few music videos from the eighties (i.e. Rick Astley), which led to some newer videos (also Rick Astley), which eventually led me to this nightly journaling.

Outside, the temperature is dropping; a snowstorm is coming our way. But inside, I'm warm (at least in heart) and feeling much happier. Journaling my thoughts and focusing my mind on Jesus gives me the strength to continue. He is my Defense against depression.

November 28, 2018

PSALM 10:17
> LORD, You have heard the desire of the humble;
> You will prepare their heart;
> You will cause Your ear to hear

I RECENTLY VISITED A WEBSITE, THE Mighty, and shared an article about chronic pain titled, "27 Things Chronic Pain Is Not." It was informative. And I took many notes. But how do I convey this message to those who do not suffer from chronic pain? How do I say, "Chronic pain is not:

> **MY CHOICE.**
> I didn't ask for this! My body broke.
>
> **"ALL IN MY HEAD."**
> Well, migraines happen in my head, but that's not what most people mean. This pain is not a part of my imagination.
>
> **ACUTE PAIN OR SLIGHT PAIN.**
> Chronic means long-lasting, lifetime. I wish it was acute and curable.

A SIMPLE CONDITION.
It's so complex that I have a hard time understanding it. So many symptoms are related to my condition, and other chronic illnesses are born from it and cause it.

SOMETHING THAT CAN BE CURED.
Again, I wish it could be. One medication worked but caused serious side effects, so I had to stop it. Other medications only relieve the symptoms somewhat. I have good days, bad days, days that have swollen feet, numb legs, or limited cognitive abilities. I never know what each day will bring.

ABOUT HAVING LOW PAIN TOLERANCE.
Somedays, the pain I go through is enough to bring the Hulk or Thor to his knees. It'll even make the devil cry and wail—an exaggeration, but my point is made.

BEING LAZY.
Too many days, I wish that my body wouldn't betray me. Then I could go on hikes, shop, walk, etc. I don't quit, but I must listen to my body. When it says no, then it means no.

VISIBLE.
I have been skilled at hiding the pain and screaming in my head. My pain is there. My exhaustion is there.

SOMETHING I'LL GROW ACCUSTOMED TO.
There's no way I can get accustomed to this. Each day, there is always a new surprise. The ebb and flow can drive me bonkers.

An easy way of life.
It is a tough thing to live with. My independence is gone. My former life is gone. Pain is a constant companion.

A natural part of aging.
Arthritis, joint pain, muscle aches—those are rites of passage. Not the bone-deep, nerve-screaming pain that never quits.

A sign of weakness.
If anything, chronic pain makes me stronger. Not physically, but in fortitude—spiritually and mentally. I learn to be strong and face it head-on.

The same for everyone who suffers.
Just as people have different body types, they also have different types of chronic pain. What I have symptom-wise will be different from another, although we can share similarities.

An excuse.
I wish—I want—I desire to do things, especially with family. But there are too many days when I can't walk, move, nor speak because of the fatigue and pain.

Predictable.
I wish it was, though. Then I could plan.

Fun.
Too many times, I have thought murderous thoughts because of the pain. Who would want this?

ONLY PHYSICAL PAIN.
It's nerve pain. It's muscle pain. It's head pain. It's the whole body screaming at the world: bones, nerves, vessels, and muscles! Even the brain!

A PLEA FOR ATTENTION.
I want to be understood, but I would never wish for pain to gain attention. People who believe that are without compassion!

FUNNY.
I may laugh at myself. But this is real, and it is serious.

AN EXCUSE TO OBTAIN NARCOTICS.
Nothing irks me more than someone who believes this, especially a doctor. Conventional narcotics do not work. I want help because I long for relief. And with the current crisis about prescription opiates, for nerve pain patients, these medications are not to be prescribed.

SOMETHING THAT I CAN IGNORE.
The more it is ignored, the more it becomes a serious problem. Ignoring it will never make it go away.

MY FAULT.
I didn't do a thing to cause this. I was healthy once. Now I'm not.

SOMETHING THAT I CAN SIMPLY "GET OVER."
Yeah. That is ridiculous. Why would someone think that? I can't just move past my pain. It's a part of me now.

THE DEFINING ASPECT OF MY IDENTITY.
Chronic pain doesn't define me. It has changed me and my life, but it hasn't changed the essence of who I am.

SOMETHING THAT MAKES ME A BAD PERSON, BAD EMPLOYEE, BAD MOM, BAD WIFE, ETC.
It is difficult to do something. Holding down a job is not feasible. My pain and fatigue won't allow a job outside the home.

CONSISTENT.
I never know how my days will begin nor end. It's never the same. Pain surprises me each day—either with its absence or with a full marching band parade.

A COMPLETELY NEGATIVE EXPERIENCE.
I've learned to slow down. I've learned to take joy in what I am able to do. I've learned to fall into God's Word even more than I had before. I've learned to listen, to love, to share. I don't see darkness; I see hope.

I've learned to humble myself, and the Lord has taught me to hear. I'm still a work in progress, but He's ever so patient with me.

November 29, 2018

---

2 CORINTHIANS 4:16-18

Therefore we do not lose heart. Even though our outward man is perishing, yet the inward man is being renewed day by day. For our light affliction, which is but for a moment, is working for us a far more exceeding and eternal weight of glory, while we do not look at things which are seen, but at the things which are not seen. For the things which are seen are temporary, but the things which are not seen are eternal.

THERE IS ONE THING THAT I do look forward to—eternal life. I will be able to run, to dance, to sing, to do many of the things I cannot do now.

Tonight, I had planned to write and record my thoughts, but I've found that my thoughts are not as coherent as they should be. For example, while talking to my oldest son this evening, I couldn't remember the word "guitar"! I had to hold my hands up and play an air guitar and make the sound of the Deliverance banjo.

Fibro fog . . . no way to say it other than: It stinks!

That is what we think when the brain fog hits. It's distasteful. It is horrendous, horrid, terrible. It's like a rotten egg marinating on hot asphalt at noon in the Nevada desert. It stinks.

And it does!

Let's see, in the space of two days, I couldn't remember "detergent," "oven," and "guitar." There were three or four more that I can't remember—and I just realized I can't remember much of the last two days either!

Maybe I overworked and overextended myself. Today, we were beginning the rearrangement of our tiny apartment to make room for our Christmas tree. This was after dealing with my editing projects, cleaning, and ordering medicine. Doesn't sound like a lot, does it?

Once, I could clean the kitchen, sweep and mop the floors, do laundry, balance the checkbook, pay bills, work on edits, homeschool, cook, and still find time to do recreational things like reading or playing a game. But not now!

If I clean the kitchen, I'm done for. The next four hours are spent recouping. If I do the laundry, I can only accomplish two loads that make it through the drying process. One load may sit in the dryer while another rests in a basket at the foot of my bed. If I cook, my day has ended before it began.

Reviewing my previous entries, I have noticed a difference. My days are waning into the bad days. I'm on the dark side of the moon. All I can do is wait and allow myself to cry. This chronic pain stuff is tough. It zaps everything from me. But I cannot lose heart, can I? I'll have to keep reading 2 Corinthians 4:16-18 again and again until I can say, "I believe what You say, Lord." Even though it seems as though the dread of winter has claimed my heart, I know that it will last only a short while. All of this is only for a moment.

Right?

December 1, 2018

PSALM 4:3-6

> But know that the LORD has set apart for Himself him who is godly;
> The LORD will hear when I call to Him.
> Be angry, and do not sin.
> Meditate within your heart on your bed, and be still. Selah

IT'S BEEN A HORRIBLE TWO DAYS. Except for one instance. At first, we were not going to stop, but we decided to swing by our local hometown pet store. My son didn't have class that day, so he went gallivanting around with us. Read that as "errands at Walmart."

While we played with the birds, he meandered to the ferrets, rats, and rabbits (aka the rodent section). He asked if he could pet a bunny. So they let him pick one to hold. I had never before seen a look of such pure joy on his face. Never had he ever felt that way about a pet. Loved and cared for them, but not like this.

So, we bought him his early Christmas present. Bunny, cage, bedding, water bottle, and dish. (We already had food.) Now Natasha (named after Marvel's Black Widow) resides happily in his room and is being completely spoiled.

I didn't mind sacrificing a few things that we needed. My son has been through a lot in his life, and he tries hard to do what is needed. Not to mention, he takes it upon himself to worry about us. He's becoming a beautiful young man of God. I love seeing him smile. It makes me forget about my pain when his joy shines.

Maybe that is how God sees us. He loves to make us happy and make us smile. He loves to see our joy shine. Maybe that is why Natasha the bunny has come into our lives. Her quirky personality brightens our lives. Even watching our youngest cat, Lord Yu, determined to make friends with Natasha is fun to see.

Think God loves to see His children become friends with one another? I think so. Maybe He sets us apart, takes us down a journey, so that our lives become intertwined with others and we become this beautiful tapestry that will hang in Heaven for all to see.

It's a beautiful thought. And all because of my son massaging my neck to relieve tension that was causing pain, which in turn led us to one more stop—since I wasn't hurting as much—which led to Natasha, and Blake's smile. And that afternoon taught me a lesson: God gives us small things to bring us joy. It keeps us humble. And it keeps pure the happiness we feel.

No, the pain hasn't disappeared, but I find that the exhaustion from that day was totally worth it. I love how God will show me His truths through the simplest of things.

December 2, 2018

HEBREWS 13:15

Therefore by Him let us continually offer the sacrifice of praise to God, that is, the fruit of our lips, giving thanks to His name.

ONE OF THE TOUGHEST THINGS TO do is to be thankful while soaked in pain. Oh, I'm sure someone would tell me about Job. But I'm no Job. I'm me. God knows me and knows I try.

Since yesterday, my feet, ankles, and legs have been swollen because I forced myself to move, even though my body was telling me no. After a series of cracks and pops in my lower spine, I had the juxtaposition of pain and numbness in my legs. It wasn't long before walking became something that was fleeing from me. Standing required every ounce of my strength.

Shall I talk about my bath? I thought that would help me some. Getting in the tub was a chore, yet not too difficult. But I was stuck. Afterward, I couldn't move my legs to climb out. Could I slither over the side? No. I had no leverage to do that. It took twenty minutes to rotate onto my stomach, rest to gain some energy, pull my legs under me, and kneel in the water. By then, I was crying from the pain that kneeling was causing.

I had placed a towel on the edge of the tub to prevent me from slipping. I eventually was able to sit on the edge, but my legs were still in the water. Now I had to figure out how to swing around. That took ten minutes to push and drag my legs out of the tub. Then I was sitting on the edge of the tub, a towel wrapped around me, and waiting. Twenty minutes ticked by before I could drag my pain-riddled and dead-legged body to the toilet. Another ten minutes, I was able to pull myself up to stand at the sink. Deodorant, lotion, powder . . .

Four to five feet away was the bed. Remember, I live in a small apartment. Our "en suite" is just a few feet from our bed. I leaned against the bed and slowly dressed.

After the hour it took to get from the tub to being dressed, I called my son to help me. I climbed into bed, and he helped me get my left leg onto the bed. Then he went and collected my Bible, my journal, pen, colored gel pens, a coloring project I was working on, and a drink.

Despite the pain and the fear I felt at being stuck, naked, in the bathroom because I couldn't move, I did find something to be thankful about. Actually, I found a few things:

1. Even though my husband was at work, I'm thankful for technology that allowed me to talk to him while struggling in the bathroom. His love and concern talked me through the ordeal.

2. My parents' teaching instilled in me to never give up and that I can always find a solution. And I did. I moved like a sloth.

3. My son wants to be a Certified Nurse Assistant before he graduates high school and then eventually work up to a nurse or paramedic. So I am his guinea pig. He practices his medical knowledge on me. Helping me move and tending to me is a part of what he will have to do in that career. And he loves to help.

4. God knows my frustrations and fears, and yet, He keeps me in His hands and sees me through it all. After I cry, He wipes my tears and bolsters my determination. He tells me, "Stay strong. Look to Me."

My future is uncertain, but I have family and God to see me through it. Pain can't conquer me. Tonight has proven that!

December 5, 2018

MALACHI 4:2

> *But to you who fear My name*
> *The Sun of Righteousness shall arise*
> *With healing in His wings;*
> *And you shall go out*
> *And grow fat like stall-fed calves.*

A NUMBER OF THINGS HAVE HAPPENED as a result of dealing with chronic pain:

1. I have forgotten what it feels like to walk and run.
2. I have accepted that pain has become a part of me. What is pain-free?
3. Days of depression are a new norm.
4. I've learned to take advantage of my good days and complete hard-pressed tasks.
5. I've forgotten what a normal life was like. That sounds pretty dire, but it's not really.

At times, it's a loud companion, but a companion, nonetheless, who has come to stay. Sometimes it brings a plus-one: depression.

I've never truly experienced depression until lately. There's a song by For King & Country—"God Only Knows"—that speaks volumes.

God only knows what I go through—what I feel—because even I, at times, have no idea how to explain or describe how I feel. The depression gets dark, and I try to find things to keep me going: my sons, my husband, my family, my pets. I try to find activities to help me: games, reading, music, writing, or painting/drawing. I'm not always successful in my distractions, but I know that it is only a matter of time before it passes. I only need to hold on for a little longer.

These are my valleys. I continue to look up, hoping to see the shining, morning mountains. There are times when it comes quickly, and I'm free of the dark thoughts. Other times, it will last for days. This last time, it happened for three days, as evident by the journal entries that are missing.

I can't write in the journal during my darkest time. There are experts who say I should, but it doesn't work for me. Have you ever seen a leaf float in a river? Eventually, it will either sink to the bottom or be caught in an eddy that brings it to shore. I'm that leaf caught in an eddy. I know I'll be brought to shore soon.

Tonight is a short entry. I don't have much to say.

So I say *adieu*, my journal. Until next time.

December 6, 2018

ISAIAH 58:8

> *Then your light shall break forth like the morning,*
> *Your healing shall spring forth speedily,*
> *And your righteousness shall go before you;*
> *The glory of the LORD shall be your rear guard.*

A REAR GUARD. IT'S NICE TO know that Someone is watching my six. Tonight, I'm thankful for a lot.

Friends. Friends that I have made through my writing, editing, and social media. They are too far away to share a cuppa with, but they are never too far to talk to.

My husband. He's the light of my life, my heart's path, the dear one who holds me and whom I adore.

I can keep on with the list. What's that hymn? "Count Your Many Blessings." When I do that, all my worries and pain fall away. Fall away as in leave me? No. But they cannot plague me. Especially the pain.

It's been two weeks—well, almost two—since I had my medication. Insurance doesn't pay for compounds, so I had to wait until I had the money to purchase it. And now I have to wait until it arrives. Hopefully, it will be soon. The medication lowers the severity of my pain. I'm sure once I get the medicine built back up in my system, the pain will no longer spiral me down into depression and color my thoughts with negativity.

Some may call it a sin to think negatively, saying that I'm taking my eyes off Jesus. I respond to them, "Who do you think is keeping me from giving in and giving up? Who do you think is keeping me from welcoming death? Jesus! That's Who."

I said before, at my weakest, I'm at my strongest.

I think people would understand if they thought about one activity they love to do: shop, work out, jog, run, swim, play baseball, etc. And then they had it suddenly taken away from them with no hope of ever gaining it back. It would be then that they would understand what chronic pain does to someone.

I have to rebuild myself. I have to rediscover myself.

And that's just a bit of it. I want and wish to be able to take my son to school activities. But I can't. And I feel like a failure. The endless loop will continue. My life is a Möbius strip. Infinitely looping . . .

When I read Isaiah, I know that sweet relief is on the horizon. I must keep my resolve and continue through the dark valley. Once I become accustomed to it, I find that it's not so dark. Dim, yes, but light will always shine in the shadows.

So, I hurt. I can't walk properly. I struggle against depression. I'm constantly exhausted. And these are my good days.

But I'm alive. I can smile and laugh. I can still see and hear. I can love. I can dream. I can live.

That's all that's important. Living. And when I live for Christ, all the problems in life are just small pebbles in my shoe. Guess I should go barefoot then. I'm up for that!

December 11, 2018

2 TIMOTHY 1:7

For God has not given us a spirit of fear, but of power and of love and of a sound mind.

FIVE DAYS. THAT'S THE LENGTH OF time between now and my last journal entry. Those five days consisted of extreme fatigue, pain, hunger, and depression. Five days of four negative words. Five days, four negative words, and zero positive words to balance me.

It was a struggle. Even now, as I recline in bed to ease my spine, I find it difficult to sit here and write in my journal. I keep reading 2 Timothy 1:7 repeatedly. Timothy was a church leader in Ephesus, and Paul's letter to him was meant to give him encouragement.

In my husband's study Bible, the chapters have headings describing what that chapter is about: "Apostolic Greeting," "The Path of a 'Good Soldier,'" "The Believer's Resource—The Scriptures," "A Faithful Servant and His Faithful Lord."

I like the last heading.

I do try to be a faithful servant, even when I feel like a servant with no direction.

I sit here, mind wandering, and feel like I have failed. How can one be of sound mind and still think a million thoughts? Is my future going to be me in a wheelchair? Is my future going to be filled with pain? Is my future going to be filled with homelessness and hunger? Is my future going to be filled with always walking this shadowed valley?

And the negative thoughts go on. How can I combat the negative?

In a wheelchair?

Maybe, maybe not. I know it doesn't matter. As long as I can get outside every once in a while, I'll be okay.

Filled with pain?

Probably so. And I'm prepared for it. Only Divine intervention will release my pain. Until then or until I'm called home, I'll accept it. It won't be easy, but that's what I'll do.

Homelessness and hunger?

I know that the future can contain the possibility when we will no longer be able to pay our rent and have even a more difficult time putting food on the table; but until then, I will not worry about the future. My God has it covered.

Shadowed valley?

I'm used to being in the shadows. And the shadows can provide cooling shade. Not only that, as I told an author friend recently, she can be the light for the world, and I can be one for the shadowed corners of the church. So, I don't mind this shadowed valley.

A sound mind. It make sense now. A sound mind holds no fear. I won't fear anything. No fear of pain. No fear of the future. Through Christ, I have power over fear. Through Christ, I have power over pain. Through Christ, I have power over the shadows.

"A Faithful Servant and His Faithful Lord" means much more now. It doesn't matter how much I falter. It doesn't matter how much pain may take away from me—even the energy to read the Bible. It doesn't matter that I worry at times or have negative thoughts. I am faithful to Jesus because I keep my eyes on Him. Being faithful doesn't mean reading every day, or pushing through pain, or not worrying. Being faithful is me not setting such thoughts above Him. Being faithful is putting Christ first.

In turn, He is faithful to me. I do not know His plans, but I trust in His timing, His path, and His guidance along this journey.

December 15, 2018

PSALM 34:17

> *The righteous cry out, and the LORD hears,*
> *And delivers them out of all their troubles.*

THERE IS ONE THING THAT I have learned about having chronic pain, fibromyalgia, and who knows what else, and that is this: writing this journal shows how debilitating this condition can be. (Can I call it a disease? I don't know. I'll have to research that.)

It was my intention to just journal my thoughts to help me through this, to accept it, to deal with it, to learn how to manage it. Then it was revealed, why not also allow others to see? So, I decided that I would have my journal printed.

Thirty days of entries, but not all consecutive days. Fibromyalgia will steal my time, my energy, my strength, and my life. I was told by my pain management specialist that winter would be a tough time for me. Boy, was he not kidding!

What started off in October as consistency has now become sporadic entries. The most days skipped so far? Five. But that is okay. This will show the reality of what happens to someone. Like now—tonight, I'm able to pick up a pen and finally write something in the journal.

I thought about reaching out to others and asking for their stories, something to insert at the back of the book. To show others that they are not alone in this fight. But I have no idea how to do that. Or how to even start!

One hurdle at a time, though. Tonight's hurdle is to write in the journal, ignore the pain, believe that tomorrow I can walk, and know that I can do some work. I only wish to know: how many times must I cry out? I guess as many times as I need to. God does not grow weary of my cries and my groans. And, boy, am I doing that tonight.

You see, I lied. I lied about having no fears. But maybe it wasn't a lie. Maybe it was me wanting to believe a deception and not knowing it was a self-deception. I do have a fear—a fear of not being able to walk. What would happen if I found myself no longer able to walk? Everything would change! Is it change I fear?

Wheelchair. Okay. I live in a second-floor apartment that isn't handicap-accessible. We can't afford to move nor to reapply for a first-floor apartment. Then there's the coping with dressing, bathing, cooking, traveling, etc., etc., etc.

Is it the future I fear? The unknown? Maybe it's not fear that I feel, but the sense of loss? Then again, after these bad days pass, I may have use of my legs again.

It's a dangerous thing to dwell on the what-ifs and maybes. The only thing I can do is cry out. Accept the help given. Live one day at a time.

What's that hymn? "One Day at a Time, Sweet Jesus"? It's been so long since I've heard it, I don't remember. I only recall the part that says, "one day at a time."

That's all I can do—trust in Him one day at a time.

December 18, 2018

1 CORINTHIANS 10:13

> *No temptation has overtaken you except such as is common to man; but God is faithful, who will not allow you to be tempted beyond what you are able, but with the temptation will also make the way of escape, that you may be able to bear it.*

I'VE LEARNED, RATHER HARSHLY, THAT WHEN my doctor says no, I should listen to her.

She told me no holiday shopping, online only. But I wanted to get out of the apartment. It wasn't a need; it was a want.

So, my husband, son, and I went and collected my mother. We went to four stores. Three of them were stores where we spent a lot of time. I had fun. It was nice to spend time with my mother as we shopped for presents. But I should have listened.

We spent five hours shopping. And I spent three days in extreme pain and still haven't recovered from it. My doctor wasn't being mean or putting limitations on me. She knew what these winter months would do to me. My condition progresses quickly, and I'm still learning about it. She wanted to prevent unneeded suffering—and I didn't listen.

But I will now.

This makes me draw a parallel to the Lord. He wants only the best for me. He isn't putting limitations on me by saying no and "obey"; He's protecting me. Keeping me from harm because He knows what will happen.

And sometimes—most times!—I do not listen. But His grace picks me back up to try again . . . and again.

Wanting to get out of the apartment, even if for a little while, was my temptation. I felt as though I needed it. I wanted it because I was envious of my sister-in-law spending time with my mom. I was jealous of seeing everyone else out and about. I wanted that, too!

And I paid a great price for my hard-headedness. It was my sin of envy that brought my pain.

Never again!

My days with Mom can be spent playing Scrabble, drinking coffee, and eating fruitcake (our homemade cake, not the store-bought) at her condo. It's those kind of days that are truly special.

The good thing about those days of pain I endured was that I could bear it. I constantly prayed and listened to God, my husband, my body. Suffering from fibromyalgia is horrible, and it isn't a bad thing to rest. It is okay to treat winter like nature behaves—sleep and rest. A new day will arrive soon—bright and alive.

December 21, 2018

ISAIAH 53:4

> Surely He has borne our griefs
> And carried our sorrows;
> Yet we esteemed Him stricken,
> Smitten by God, and afflicted.

AS THE CHRISTMAS HOLIDAYS QUICKLY APPROACH, I can understand how people become depressed. Some are alone because they have no family or their family lives far away. Some are poor, and they cannot have a feast like some people. Some have been burned by the church and have no house of worship to attend. Some are house-bound because of health reasons.

As I have said before, having this condition affords me a deeper empathy toward others. I cannot shop or stroll through the places that are decorated for the holidays. I cannot find the energy to make my favorite Christmas foods or try out new recipes.

It's hard to keep up the strength that is needed. It's hard to keep up a façade. At times, I want to crumple. And those are the times that I should. There is no shame when I crumple under the pressure and pain.

When I allow myself to stop and let the pain run its course, I know that at the end, I will be stronger for it. If not physically, then emotionally, mentally, and spiritually. I know that God will hold me until I can stand.

It's a blessing to have that faith. And I feel saddened when I think of those who deny Him.

Speaking of blessings, tonight Nate was secretly gifted a twenty-five-dollar gift card to a local grocery store. We can have our Christmas ham now! And I have just the recipe for it, courtesy of The Food Network and Ina Garten.

As I write this, I realized that as the days grow shorter, so do my entries. It takes a lot to write down my thoughts. Even typing is difficult, since I've been experiencing Raynaud's Syndrome—a fancy name for blue fingers due to poor circulation. Joy, joy—one more symptom to manifest.

I find myself wondering if I should look at moving to a warmer climate, maybe somewhere coastal, but I still hesitate because I don't feel called to anywhere else—at least not yet. Maybe soon, I can go back to the pool, especially since it's indoors and heated! Aqua therapy does help.

It will probably be a while again before I make another entry. Christmas week will be a vacation for me. Rest. Recuperation. Reflection. I need those three in order to keep going. And my prayer tonight—as I look at my prayer wall and remember those listed in prayer—is that I can find some sort of support group or fellowship or friendship. Not just for me, but for my family. Living here has become lonely. Having friends to share life with makes things better.

But either/or, I'm content. The Lord is with me, and I have the love of my family with me.

Intermission

MATTHEW 1:18-23 (KJV)

Now the birth of Jesus Christ was on this wise: When as his mother Mary was espoused to Joseph, before they came together, she was found with child of the Holy Ghost.

Then Joseph her husband, being a just man, and not willing to make her a public example, was minded to put her away privily.

But while he thought on these things, behold, the angel of the Lord appeared unto him in a dream, saying, Joseph, thou son of David, fear not to take unto thee Mary thy wife: for that which is conceived in her is of the Holy Ghost.

And she shall bring forth a son, and thou shalt call his name JESUS: for he shall save his people from their sins.

Now all this was done, that it might be fulfilled which was spoken of the Lord by the prophet, saying,

Behold, a virgin shall be with child, and shall bring forth a son, and they shall call his name Emmanuel, which being interpreted is, God with us.

December 30, 2018

PSALM 107:20
> *He sent His word and healed them,*
> *And delivered them from their destructions.*

CHRISTMAS HAS COME AND GONE. THIS year marked the first year the majority of my family was together for the holiday in six years. And Christmas was what I expected it to be: fun, laughter, sibling squabbles, love of children, love of family, and, of course, the celebration of Christ's birth.

The days after were painful. My merriment came at a cost, but it was worth it. Those days of pain offered a time of reflection.

I don't debate the history of Christmas or why the twenty-fifth of December was chosen. I always said that if people were interested in the truth, they can find it with a little research.

No. My reflection was on Christ. A death that was gruesome and yet glorious. He chose to die for me—and each and every person born and unborn. God came down and walked among us. He became one of us. He died for us. He lives for us. For me.

Too many times, people want to quantify God. They want to reduce Him to human characteristics. They try to dismiss Him. They deny Him. He created the world, the air we breathe, the stars we see, the universe, and beyond. Of all His creations, we are His most precious.

People ask, "Then why does He allow suffering and pain to exist?" I can't answer that—not fully. But why do they ask me about God? They know the answer: "We live in a fallen world." They know the reason behind why we live in a fallen world.

They ask me because they want an excuse. They ask others because they want an excuse. They never ask God.

The answer to that question—"Why do You allow suffering and pain?"—is different for everyone. For me, it slows me down. Allows me to reflect on His Word. Makes me lean on Him and not myself. Has me relying on the love of my family and knowing that I am loved. And probably helps someone who is suffering as I am. And maybe if they have not accepted Christ, they will see His love for them through me.

It frightens me to know what lies in wait for those who have denied Christ. I have never understood how one could not believe when belief in Him is so simple. That's all it takes. No alms. No deeds to complete. No absolutions. No donations. No sacrifice—no!

There is one sacrifice—the sacrifice of your old self. With Christ, our souls are made new. He delivers us from our destruction. Whether that is physically, emotionally, and/or mentally, it definitely means He delivers us from our spiritual destruction.

He sends His Word and heals us. Whether it is physically, emotionally, and/or mentally healed, He does heal us spiritually.

Doctors can do only so much to heal someone. Inflammation coursed through my body after Christmas. After trigger point injections, I was put on a step-down dose of steroids, which gradually reduced the inflammation. One of my meds was increased to two pills a day for two weeks. And a request for aqua therapy was sent to my insurance. And that is the extent of what my doctor can do.

Whether I am eventually healed or will live with this condition for the rest of my life is beside the point. Instead of dwelling on my "cannots," I have learned to work with my "cans." I can do some things. So, I do them.

Short shopping trips—an hour max, only two days a week. I can do that.

Scheduling my time for work, writing, homeschooling, paying bills, adhering to the schedule—I can do that!

Cooking only one dish a day or every other day and using quick fixes or frozen foods—I can do that.

Using life hacks—I can do that.

Resting often. Never pushing myself. Saying no when I need to. I can do that.

Accepting help when it is given—I can do that.

Being positive brings healing. The less tense I am, the less pain I have. Life is to be enjoyed. And I cannot enjoy life when I am "woeing up" the negative.

Since I love to read, I'm taking the time to read a book or two a week. It doesn't matter that I can no longer read a book in a day. If it takes me three to four days to read one, more joy for me. I'm living in a fictional world that much longer. Or I'm marinating in the wise words written in a nonfiction that I delve into.

Just as Christ's words have healing, so do these positive words in my life: I can.

P.S. Quick fixes and frozen food have become a time-saver and life-saver. There are many out there that I cannot have because of the ingredients used, but I found a few: frozen pasta meals, frozen meatballs, corn dogs, etc. Quick dinner fixes that even my non-chef family can handle.

P.P.S. I've begun to experience Raynaud's Syndrome, and the inflammation causes my fingers to hurt to the point that writing, or typing, is nearly impossible. I found fingerless gloves, but I also found arthritis gloves at Walgreens. I was looking for compression gloves; and when I saw these, which were less expensive, I decided to try them. And they work! They reduce the pain and warm my fingers! I also bought an elbow Copperfit sleeve for the times my elbow aches.

When it came to taking my meds, I relabeled a pill box and divvied my pills for the day: breakfast, lunch, supper, bedtime, nighttime. No meds were missed. No meds forgotten. All taken on time. If it works and it helps, I use it!

January 12, 2019

JAMES 4:7

Therefore submit to God. Resist the devil and he will flee from you.

IF MY PAIN WAS THE DEVIL and I fled from it, then I would not have this thorn in my life. But pain isn't the devil. Some pain can be caused by him, but most are just a way of life in this fallen world. And for me, as a Christian, I see it as a small moment in my existence that allows me to draw closer to God and truly see His majestic power and love. Funny how pain—that ugly, black menace—allows for beauty and light to shine.

It has been almost two weeks since my last journal entry. There were so many instances when I wished to pick up the book and write. At times, I held pen and journal in hand with thoughts swirling, but fatigue and pain kept me from being able to write.

Too many times, I've come to that cusp of giving up, throwing it all into the chasm, and falling away from this world. Only two things kept me from going that horrible distance: 1) it would have taken too much effort and 2) it would be painful no matter what I did.

With a heavy heart, I admit that it wasn't the thought of leaving my family behind. After all we've been through, I knew that they would eventually heal and that God would take care of them. It was the thought of God that stopped me. If anything, I desired to be with Him where there would no longer be any pain. There were no Scripture or verses or words that stopped me. It was more. More than those two thoughts I had. An unseen Force guided me away, and I was helpless to resist. Then I slept.

Until someone experiences pain that is beyond description, they cannot truly understand. Imagine flu-like aches multiplied by twenty and then pins and electric rods inserted into your joints—every single one!

Until someone experiences fatigue that is beyond words, they cannot fully empathize. Imagine having three to four days of no sleep and no energy, but you have to keep pushing on. That is only a fraction of what those with chronic pain experience.

Now add nausea, irritable bowels, and depression to the recipe.

No wonder many of us, especially those with no support, eventually give up and wish to die. We want sunshine. We get darkness and isolation. We want friendship. We get loneliness. We want fellowship. We get pushed aside and forgotten.

There are so many dreams I have—not the typical ones like a house, or no more bills, or becoming a well-known author. No, my dream is to have days where I'm sitting with a friend sharing a cup of tea or a cup of coffee. I wish for a "cuppa friend."

Some days, I want a friend who would let me cry on her shoulder and know that I cry because I need to release tension and pent-up emotions. I don't want to cry in front of my husband. That would worry him needlessly—but then, my husband is my best friend. My confidant. My true heart and love. He would know that I cry because I'm tired, frustrated, and lost.

Chronic illness steals so much, and learning how to cope and to rediscover myself is difficult and long. Putting the old me behind is tough. And that's when I have to resist the devil, who would delight in me giving in and giving up.

When I completely submitted to God that I was tired, exhausted, and ready to give up, He quieted my mind. He had me by the hand, and I was led away from that chasm. It isn't easy and never will be. But only through Jesus will I continue to survive. Despite the pain and fatigue and sickness, I know I can continue—little by little, day by day.

January 18, 2019

JAMES 5:14-15

> *Is anyone among you sick? Let him call for the elders of the church, and let them pray over him, anointing him with oil in the name of the Lord.*

AND THE PRAYER OF FAITH WILL save the sick, and the Lord will raise him up. And if he has committed sins, he will be forgiven.

I've heard many people say it. I've read where many people wrote it. What did I do to deserve this?

In most cases, nothing.

Thinking back and looking at how I felt years ago, I recognize some of the symptoms of fibromyalgia. To me, back then, it was tiredness from worrying. I was a young widow with two sons and no one to help me. Even the church had failed me.

Back then, I attributed the pain to overdoing the physical labor needed around our home. I see small things that I always pushed through. I couldn't tell anyone because, frankly, they wouldn't have listened. They would have said, "Push through it"; "You need to exercise more"; "You need to get rid of your pets"; and the list goes on.

So, I suffered in silence.

Then when I accepted Nate's proposal, I noticed a constant pain in my neck, shoulders, and back. Even through our wedding, it was there. It came and went. The aches spread, fluctuating in intensity. Never too bad. More annoying than anything.

Skip to the present, and now, after learning to recognize the signs of a flare-up, I know that my fibromyalgia began in my mid-thirties, and I had no one there for support. Even now, in a new place, we haven't found a church home yet. Of the three that we have visited, one became a probable home—until my sickness hit.

My days normally begin after noon because of my body. It takes longer to dress now. My sleep is interrupted by pain. I'm in a state of exhaustion. And as I travel through this wintertime, I can only dream of going to church on Sunday.

But they probably have forgotten us. For over a year, after battling a respiratory virus that kept me homebound for three months and then having extreme pain from the fibromyalgia and many ER visits because of the chronic migraines, no one visited. No one called. No one reached out to ask how we were doing.

I asked once to be put on the prayer list. Two weeks later, the pastor sent me a message asking how we were doing. We attended Sunday worship.

Then I fell ill again. And no one cared enough to ask what happened, how we were doing, or to even say "hi."

Being forgotten, misunderstood, mislabeled, and ignored heightens the symptoms of a chronic illness. I would love to be prayed over by a church, particularly by the elders (deacons).

I turn to an online women's fellowship, but what about my husband and my son? As caregivers, they must not be forgotten either! They have taken on themselves that which I cannot do. They balance work and school as they help me. I pray for them, always. I pray that God gives them strength and guides them. Their love sees me through!

Our search for a church continues. God will lead us to one in His timing. We continue to look to Him in all things.

I'm going back through physical therapy, but that's okay. It continues to help me. I have to use the dreaded cane. But that's okay. I plan to paint verses on it and spread God's Word as I hobble throughout town.

I may revisit pain and be stuck in a bed at times, but God will see us through this. As long as I keep God first, I know that things will turn out okay. It won't be as I imagined, but God's plan is always better than my imagination.

January 27, 2019

ISAIAH 26:3
You will keep him in perfect peace,
Whose mind is stayed on You,
Because he trusts in You.

FROM PHYSICAL THERAPY TO A NEW medication, I find myself struggling to keep on going. I'm not giving up; but I'm tired; I struggle; I want only to rest . . . and rest and rest.

Inflammation inside my body created a new problem for me. At first, I thought I must have caught a cold or developed an infection that caused my breasts to hurt and a lymph node to swell. It turns out it was fibromyalgia causing the problems. And on top of that, I discovered why the tops of my thighs were constantly breaking out into a rash.

I learned that because I suffer from interstitial cystitis (IC) that many products on the market would affect not only my skin, but my bladder, too. I went to a website: www.rosebedwomenshealth.wordpress.com.

The blogger talks about her discoveries, and I realized it wouldn't hurt to try some of her techniques and suggestions: cotton underwear, loose clothing, eliminating soaps with perfumes and dyes, eliminating detergents with the same. Even some lotions were causing problems, as well as perfumes.

My solution for soap is Dove™ bars for sensitive skin. Lotion is shea butter that I bought at Bath and Body Works. Sometimes, I add an essential oil to it for fragrance. I also buy natural products from a place in Sioux Falls, South Dakota (marniesbodycare.com). It takes only a little bit of adjusting my lifestyle to get a handle on the IC rash.

As for my breast pain, because the inflammation was so bad, I was put on a low dose of gabapentin. I do not respond well to high doses and show a heightened sensitivity to gabapentin. But the medicine caused the pain to recede, although I got splitting headaches from it. Thankfully, I'm on the medication for only a few days.

Because of the new medicine, the flare-ups, and pain, I stay exhausted. And I sleep. And when I sleep, before I completely drift to those dreams, my mind centers on Christ. I'm not thinking thoughts. I'm not wondering. I'm in that perfect peace, knowing that even though I was too exhausted to read the Bible, His words still came to me. Even though I was too exhausted to speak, He knew my heart and thoughts.

I'm reminded that this is for only a season. I can let it break me or make me stronger. If I keep my eyes on Him, then I know this will strengthen me. And the best part is that His peace wraps over into my dreams. There are times in my dreams where I can run, walk, and even race. I can do things that seem only a dream in real life. That gives me hope that someday I may be like the person I am in my dream.

March 20, 2019

PSALM 91:1-2

> *He who dwells in the secret place of the Most High*
> *Shall abide under the shadow of the Almighty.*
> *I will say of the LORD, "He is my refuge and my fortress;*
> *My God, in Him I will trust."*

I PURPOSELY IGNORED WRITING IN THE journal until now. My intention was to be able to chronicle a month or more of what happens. And it's been a doozy.

Living in Iowa gives me harsh winters. And after being told that I would suffer greatly this winter, I believed it. It took a while, but I did.

Pain can be quite strange. At a recent check-up, I was told I had one of the worst cases of fibromyalgia. I can count on seven types of pain. They can range from experiencing only two or three every day or all seven.

I have seven constant daily companions.

Randomly Moving Pain and Rattled Nerves. Randomly moving pain is exactly what it sounds like. The dull, achy pain migrates throughout the body and particularly loves the joints—every joint—even joints in the toes! Rattled nerves are the hardest to explain. The all-over-ache likes to hold hands with nausea, dizziness, or anxiety.

Sometimes, it's a group activity. Anxiety speeds my heart and breathing, which induces an asthma attack. This, in turn, causes me to tense. My muscles contract, and the pain intensifies. The pain rises and rattles my nerves. And . . . complete circle.

The clue to defeating these vicious and demonic cycles is to deny it a link. So, I take deep breaths. In through the nose. Out through the mouth. I think upon a verse of Scripture, a song, or a pleasant image. Mine is sunshine upon a flower—a daisy, standing tall in the grass, and dandelion seeds blowing around. It's a constant battle, but one I can continue to fight when I realize I'm not alone.

The other pains usually visit at the same time—my uninvited guests.

Sparkler Burns.
These are pains that feel like pin-pricks that are triggered when touched or scratched.

Allodynia.
This is the painful response to something that is normally not harmful—for example, running a fingertip across the tabletop or across a textured lampshade.

Hyperalgesia.
This is different from allodynia. Hyperalgesia is an increased response to painful stimuli. With Allodynia, some clothing can be painful, such as waffle-weave material. With hyperalgesia, a prick from a rose's thorn is multiplied by a hundred. A stubbed toe or a bump of the elbow can send me to my knees, curled up and bawling from the pain it causes.

PARESTHESIA.
This is the one that bothers me the most. Numbness, tingling, and pins and needles that have no discrimination. They pick wherever on the body to visit.

KNIFE IN THE VOODOO DOLL.
I hate and like this companion. I hate how it feels, but I like its moniker. This pain slices and stabs through me. An invisible ninja has descended upon me and thrusts his katana into my body!

It has been these seven pains that I've dealt with these past two months. Coupled with ptosis (droopy eyelid) from a failed Botox treatment for my chronic migraines and being newly diagnosed with sacroiliitis, which is the inflammation of the sacroiliac joint located on either side of the lower spine. All this causes depression to set in at times. Sometimes, I just want to give up. Too tired to keep going. Too tired to give in. Too much pain to fight back. Too much pain to lie down.

It feels a lot like a lose-lose situation. That's when those I call friends step in. Even a random message from an acquaintance reaches me.

"How are you today?"

"Thinking about you."

"May I pray for you today?"

"You're in my prayers."

"Just checking on you, friend."

It takes only one to bring me back from the brink. God sends them my way. Even those who are not believers. Their concern for me is just as valid as my brothers and sisters in Christ.

When that fails to dim the pain, I open the Bible or read from a submission on my computer. God's Word pulls me in and hides me away from the world and its pain. I'm safe there in His Word. He's my Refuge. I'm able to gain strength from His protection. He's my Fortress.

Soon, my pain lessens, and I can return to the world. His Word still blazes in my mind, but I trust that God will see to my needs.

My days can meld into one and into another until I can't remember one day from the next. My days may never start until after everyone else's is half over. My days may be slow like the tortoise, while all else is fast like the hare.

My life is different now. But I appreciate it all the more. My life isn't to compete with others. It isn't to wish for more or be unhappy with the present. This is my life.

I learn to deal with the pain, fatigue, and myriad ailments. I learn what foods help and what will harm. I learn shortcuts to help me in my daily life. I learn my limitations and to take it one day at a time. I learn to listen to my body and to others, and, most importantly, I learn to listen to God. I trust in Him and know that in His time, this suffering will bring good and will end.

April 2019 to the Future

Mark 4:39

> *Then He arose and rebuked the wind, and said to the sea, "Peace, be still!" And the wind ceased and there was a great calm.*

I sat on this entry for a long time. Thoughts would come and go. Ideas filtered through and then became lost to the darkness of time. No matter how many times I thought about doing this last entry, I could not make myself pick up my pen . . . until now.

Life is always in flux. Ever-moving. Ever-changing. Totally unpredictable. One day can give me ultimate relief and strength—even the dream of being healed. The next day, I am driven to my knees, crying out and begging God for healing and for strength. It is those days when I'm immobile, riddled with torturous pain, mind numb to words, that I reach out to my friends and family. I ask for prayer. I ask that they put me on a prayer list. And I keep them updated.

Someone's journey through a chronic illness or condition should never be traveled alone. We are social creatures. We crave human contact—whether it's a touch or a voice or a message. We want to know and believe that we are not alone. Because we are such emotional creatures, we will have an oscillating wave of jumbled feelings. We are caught in a storm of life's making.

As I sit here writing this entry, my mind sometimes drifts to the upcoming days and a business trip to South Carolina. Then I think about my mom and how she strives to help me as much as possible. I think about my husband and how he never leaves my side, even when my bad attitude arises. I think about my sons and how proud they make me. Eventually, I think about all the blessings Jesus has given me, the small and large.

Growing up, I attended Good Hope Baptist Church in Batesville, Mississippi. That church, with its gleaming pews and golden stained-glass windows, has embedded itself in my memories. It was a happy place for me.

Many Sundays, we sang an old hymn, "Count Your Blessings."

"When upon life's billows you are tempest tossed,
When you are discouraged, thinking all is lost,
Count your many blessings, name them one by one,
And it will surprise you what the Lord hath done."

If I counted, named, and listed every blessing God has given me, there would not be enough ink and paper in the world to contain them all. Little, small, great, and tall—so many blessings abound.

Knowing that for every pain I feel, I can name three blessings has helped me through my days and nights.

That one spot on my lower spine spikes pain throughout my body—I live; I have a soft pillow; I have a bed.

My bones ache—I have a sweet pet; I can see; I feel the wind.

My knee constantly hurts—I can still walk; I have books; I can listen to music.

I'm extremely exhausted—I can dream; I have clean water; I feel loved. And so forth . . .

Up and down with the waves, in and out with the tide, tossed about in the storm—none of this matters if I keep my eyes on Jesus and His blessings.

Mark 4:39 is my favorite verse. Not only does it show Jesus calming the sea, but it also shows He calmed the storm within the disciples. Not only did He command the wind, but He also commanded the direction of their hearts.

Life gives us storms. Jesus calms them for us. No matter how many times the storm arrives, Jesus is there, by my side, through it all.

As I learn more about fibromyalgia, I become better at dealing with its symptoms. I was even told I have a "yet to be diagnosed" autoimmune disease, but the inflammation in my body prevents them from knowing what tests to run in order to pinpoint it.

But that's okay. I have begun to adjust my diet in hopes of reducing the inflammation. I am determined to help my doctor, yet my eyes remain on the one true Physician. He sees me through this storm. He calms the waters around me. He guides me through this unknown.

I do not know what lies ahead, but I take it one day at a time. Reminds of the song I heard growing up, "One Day at a Time, Sweet Jesus."

That's all I can really hope for—just one day. And when I lie down to sleep, I pray for "one more day."

AUTHOR'S AFTERWORD

THESE JOURNAL ENTRIES WERE THE HARDEST thing for me to write; and then when I decided to share them, I was afraid to show the world what I thought. It is easy for me to create and share stories; but when it comes to sharing intimate feelings, it is something that was foreign to me.

Every day, I battle depression, pain, fatigue, and loss of hope. Every day, I overcome it. It never completely fades away. And it never will in this realm of life. I may not have gone into detail about the depression, but it is something that many of us who deal with chronic pain feel. We stand, so many times, on the brink, on that edge of the chasm, on that ledge.

Pain colors our perception. It colors our outlook. It colors our thinking. What was once bright and colorful has become dark and black. Many of us succumb to that lie that ending it all would be better. But when the tears are flowing and the pain won't cease assaulting us, death is all we crave. Many of us can turn away because we find more to live for compared to what we would die for.

Sometimes, it is a song, a message from family or friends, an email, a smile, or even a touch that brings us back to the living world. Sometimes, it is a memory of brighter days.

When our lives are transformed into something that we don't understand, it becomes too hard to navigate by ourselves. It is good to know that we are not alone. Technology offers the chance to connect with others, either through social media or through online apps.

So, reader, if you are one of us who suffers from pain, please find us online. Send an email. Connect. You are not alone in this struggle and fight. Reader, if you know of a friend or family member who suffers from pain, please reach out to them. Don't offer advice. Don't offer solutions. Just offer a smile or a funny story or a meme to brighten the day. Small things are the strongest weapon against depression and pain.

Our lives will consist of ups and downs, valleys and mountains, dry land and deep seas. It helps knowing that we don't journey this life alone.

FOODS AND DIET PLANS

I'M ON A STRICT, BUT NOT too strict, diet plan. Because I suffer from chronic migraines, I must watch what I eat and what ingredients are used in foods. Because I have interstitial cystitis, there are certain foods that I must avoid. Listed below are the "Migraine Diet" and "IC Diet" that I follow.

MIGRAINE DIET

This is a list of foods, beverages, and additives that are thought to trigger migraine symptoms in some people. I found that I am quite sensitive to these and must avoid them at all costs. Not all people respond the same way, so my triggers may not be triggers for you. The only way to know for sure is to use the process of elimination.

Monosodium glutamate	Aspartame
Sodium caseinate	Hydrolyzed proteins
Autolyzed yeast	Fatty foods
Aged or blue cheese	Red wine or beer
Smoked, cured, or pickled meat	Soy sauce, miso
Processed meats/food	Chocolate
Yeast and foods containing yeast	Tomato, tomato sauce, tomato paste
Fermented foods	Caffeine

Go to the National Headache Foundation website for more information on foods and diet plans for migraine sufferers.

The next table shows the list for IC/PBS (Interstitial Cystitis/Painful Bladder Syndrome). This is a more restrictive diet and one that is quite hard for me to follow. I love strawberries and tomatoes. So when I break away from my diet, I pay the price. Again, not everyone responds the same way, but using the process of elimination is beneficial in discovering what you can and cannot eat.

BLADDER FRIENDLY	TRY IT	CAUTION
Water, blueberry/pear juice, milk, tea, non-dairy creamers	Low-acid orange juice, baby fruit juice, low-acid decaf coffee, decaf soda	Alcohol, carbonated water, cranberry/orange juice, regular coffee, sodas, diet sodas, sports/energy drinks
Whole wheat bread, white bread, most cereals, grains, pasta, rice, homemade soup/broth	Rye/sourdough bread, instant hot cereal, amaranth grain, non-MSG canned soups	Processed/fortified breads, sweetened/fortified cereals, soy flour, prepared/boxed pasta, boxed rice dishes, bouillon/canned soups, packaged soups
Almonds, cashews, peanuts, butter, canola/olive/corn/safflower oils, homemade salad dressing	Macadamia, pecans, walnuts, mayonnaise, tahini, sunflower seeds, butter-flavored shortening	Filberts, hazelnuts, pistachios, most salad dressings

Foods and Diet Plans

BLADDER FRIENDLY	TRY IT	CAUTION
Eggs, poultry, fish, beef, seafood, lamb, pork, whey powder, liver	Non-soy veggie burgers, corned beef, non-cured sandwich meats, bacon, MSG-free sausage	Cured meats, canned crab meat, hot dogs, most sausage, smoked fish, soy products
American/mozzarella/feta and ricotta cheeses, cream cheese, most ice cream, whipped cream	Blue cheese/brie/sharp cheddar/edam cheeses, buttermilk, sour cream, yogurt	Soy products, citrus or chocolate flavored ice cream, processed cheeses
Gala, Pink Lady apples, applesauce, blueberries, coconut, date, pears, watermelon, honeydew	Bananas, raspberries, cherries, figs, mango, peaches, plums, raisins	Cranberries, citrus fruits, grapes, kiwi, nectarines, pineapple, strawberries
Avocado, most beans, broccoli, brussels sprouts, carrots, cauliflower, celery, cucumber, green beans, kale, spinach, bok choy, lettuce, mushrooms, potatoes, pumpkin, squash	Lima beans, kidney beans, bell peppers, olives, cooked leeks, cooked onions, low acid/homegrown tomatoes	Chili peppers, raw onions, pickles, sauerkraut, soybeans, tomato, tomato sauces, tomato juice, tofu

For more information and a more detailed look at this diet, visit: www.ic-diet.com.

TESTIMONIES

THE FOLLOWING PAGES ARE TESTIMONIES FROM other people who suffer from chronic pain, chronic illnesses, and autoimmune diseases. I had asked for people to tell me their stories to put into this book. Knowing the different stories, the different lives out there, help all of us who have had our lives forever changed by an illness, and some of these illnesses are invisible.

I hope you can find encouragement from their words.

MELINDA GREEN

MY LIFE DEALING WITH FIBROMYALGIA HAS been a major journey. I know some people argue that there are different stages of fibromyalgia, and then some say that is not true. Then you have some that argue that fibromyalgia is not a progressive illness; well, I've come to say that it is progressive.

The reason for my argument is because progressive is defined as "moving forward, advancing, and continuing steadily by increments."

I was officially diagnosed with the illness in 2007. During that time, I was able to work, travel with my job, attend school full-time trying to complete my master's in Psychology—basically, living life. I dealt with some stiffness of the joints but nothing major. As the years progressed, the stiffness turned into "barely could walk." My joints began to lock up, but I was still able to maintain and continue to work.

Then in 2015, I went from a person who could walk to a person who had to use a walker, had tremors, had severe muscle weakness in my hands and legs, and loss of vision in one eye. Living with this chronic illness has not only caused me not to work since 2015, it also caused major difficulties in my home life. I went from making a healthy salary to now living under the poverty level, barely making it from one month to the next. Not only has it caused a major shift in my finances, but I also went from a person who was independent to being dependent on not only the system but also on others for day-in and day-out help.

I remember one day feeling so alone, I had to make a choice of how much I would continue to let this illness take from me without trying to find a way to fight back. I encourage people to work through the pain, which is something I have to do on a daily basis just to have some form of a life and some form of happiness. I had to learn to make the best out of my present situation. I had to learn to shift my thinking, which sounds crazy because when you are in so much pain day-in and day-out, it is hard to think about anything.

I began to lean more on God as my Source. I developed a hobby that I would not have thought in a million years I could ever do—I learned how to get into a healthy online community as well as started a website page, Christian Women Dealing with Chronic Pain. I learned how to balance my activities. I knew that when it rained or was cold that I would be miserable, but I learned how to pace myself. I learned how to shop online (a blessing to the chronically ill); basically, what I did was learn how to live the best life I could while dealing with fibro and the multiple things that came with it.

Presently, I am doing okay with fibromyalgia. Many of us have degenerative arthritis, so now I am dealing with my knees slipping and gout; but outside of that, my spirits are great most days and, believe it or not, it does help with the pain. I believe I am using mind-over-matter; but whatever I am doing lately is working, and the pain is not as intense as it had been in the past.

Melinda Green is the founder and admin of the Facebook group, "Christian Women Dealing with Chronic Pain (Fibromyalgia, Diabetes, etc.).

TONI HIBBERD-JUDKINS

I'M SITTING HERE PREPARING FOR MY next surgery. Is everything in order? Did I forget anything? What will I need in the house when I can't get out for the weeks required to recover? Did I handle all my work clients properly? Did I get all my bills paid, so I can just relax and recover? Preparing for yet another procedure is comparable to going on vacation. The to-do list seems quite similar! Did I pack enough toiletries? Did I forget anything?

Mind you, having a surgery or procedure is not new. I have been through so many before, I kind of know the drill. I still get a little pre-surgical anxiety, if there is such a thing. Having control over the things I do have control over always helps me. After all, I will be put out for this procedure. It is a position where I have zero control. So, to put things in order the best I can beforehand has always been helpful for me. A time to prepare.

Before I knew it, my surgery was over; and this time, it required a short, overnight stay in the hospital. I hardly remember my car ride home. I do believe they kind of push people out the door these days. Nonetheless, I was excited to get out of there and into the comforts of my own home. My pups were excited that Mommy was home, and I soon settled in to begin my road to recovery.

I have a great sister, who just so happens to be a retired nurse. She had just relocated to the area and offered to take me to my post-op appointments and help in any way she could. There is something to be said about family. I am very blessed to have a good one. Yes, we all have our quirks and shortcomings, but at the end of the day, we know we can count on each other.

I am a single woman in my early fifties. This was no time to be scouting for a man. Besides, I was trusting God was preparing the best fit in a man for me. I continue to trust that He is working on that. But for now, I will leave it in His hands and take up my sister's offer to help me out.

The weeks of recovery seemed to go very slow. I had prepared so well for my healing process, and everything was in order. The only thing I did not count on is what I was going to do while I was recovering. Since I was on crutches and a full leg cast on my right foot, driving was out of the question! Weeks turned into months; and by that time, I was growing very impatient. I was ready to be better; my patience was gone, and I was ready to resume my life as I knew it.

Each day seemed to be longer than the day before. I felt down and had little hope. I was asking myself if this was ever going to end! At my most recent check-up, I questioned my orthopedic doctor, who had stated this was to be a six-to-eight-week recovery, why it was taking so long. He simply stated, "If I had told you recovery was going to take up to sixteen weeks or more, you would not have gone through with it." His words exactly. Hurt and angered by his comment, I left his office feeling betrayed, angry, and my blood ready to boil. I can honestly say it took days before I could wrap my head around what he said.

On the third day after learning I had weeks, possibly months, before I would be weight-bearing or walking, much less driving, I reached for my Bible. While most people may have reached for their Bible in advance, I was not one of those people. Ironically, I have many lady friends who also love Jesus. I reached out to them to ask where would be a good place to start my reading. It was decided that Psalms and Proverbs would be good reads for where I was.

Stuck in a chair, not able to walk and feeling alone in this world, I began my quest. But first, I had to get over the fact that most women in their fifties typically have a husband to care for them, don't they? I had my pity party, along with my nineteenth nervous breakdown, and finally decided that was not getting me anywhere. God has not yet sent such a person for me; however, I still felt like there should have been such a person. Oh well, maybe someday. Not sure why I always think God should have sent me somebody to help me along in this world. But I still do.

One of my favorite sayings has always been, "Everything happens for a reason." Who would have ever thought that I could heal my heart while recovering from a surgery on a limb! But that is exactly what happened. Without the power and strength of Jesus, I don't think I could have gotten through that time. He has given me faith, strength, hope, encouragement, truth, and so much more.

I eventually healed physically. I went through physical therapy to regain strength to walk again. Before I knew it, I was back walking, driving, and participating in my life again. Wow, what a learning experience it was!

I kept all my post-op appointments as I was supposed to. Although, I never felt like I got better. My pain had actually become worse than before my procedure, and this time it had cropped up in a new area. I was told by my doctor, "There is nothing else I can do." The whole time, I was under the impression I was going to get better; this pain will finally subside. But I was mistaken. It was not meant to be.

I had to level with the fact that this is how my life is going to be. It is a harsh reality when you sit down and realize life will never be the same. Every single step I take is going to cause me pain. Now I am not a young woman, but there are things in life I still like to do! I think everyone wants to feel productive, worthwhile, relevant, and functioning in life. How do I obtain that, given my current situation?

I set out to do just that. I went back to the things I read and wrote about many months ago in that chair. Relying upon "everything happens for a reason." God is still in control. There are days that I have to mentally prepare to even make a simple trip to the grocery or attend a function. The biggest thing that has helped me has been mind over matter. Yes, this pain is going to be present. I trust that God will provide the strength I need. Even if that strength is getting me though a simple trip to the grocery.

He has provided this strength one hundred percent of the time. No matter what level my pain is, He has seen me through. He has seen me through on days when my pain is so unbearable, I didn't think I could take one more step. But somehow, I was able.

I keep praying for a miraculous healing. So far, the miraculous part has happened only on the inside. It has not decreased my pain at all. However, my perception and approach to how I live has changed dramatically.

All of this has been a true testimony to the fact that all things are possible through Christ Jesus. I would like to challenge anyone who has had a similar experience to never give up. Let go and let GOD. Many, many days (still today), I have literally got down in the floor on my knees and asked for His help. Trust in the Lord with ALL YOUR HEART. He hears our plea. He hears our prayers even when they are in the form of tears.

Toni Hibberd-Judkins lives in Fort Myers, Florida, and is an active member on the Facebook group, "Christian Women Dealing with Chronic Pain (Fibromyalgia, Diabetes, etc.)."

LESLIE L. MCKEE

OCTOBER 26, 1994, IS A DAY I will never forget. It's the day I was hit by a car. It's also the day I began my battle with chronic pain and fibromyalgia, though it took me ten years to finally get a diagnosis.

I have been a Christ-follower since I was a child, and I certainly praised God that I survived the accident, especially when the cop told me someone had been killed in that same location in a similar accident about a week prior. However, I won't lie. I have questioned God a lot over the years, and I still do, at times. Why me? Why do I have plans for my life that my body tells me I can no longer do? Why can't I have something with a cure, instead of something people scoff at because I look perfectly fine on the outside, despite the pain I feel on the inside? While I still don't have the answers to these and other questions, I've come to realize that God still has a plan for me. That didn't change on October 26, 1994. His plans are just different than mine, but that's not a bad thing.

I've realized that I've achieved dreams I had growing up—just in a slightly different way than I originally envisioned. I now recognize that God can, and will, use every situation (good or bad) for His good. I've also acknowledged just how much I need God in my life, which is something that wasn't easy to admit, as I've always been independent. I don't like to rely on others or ask for help. I don't want to be viewed as weak. But I'm reminded of the following verse: "Each time he said, 'My grace is all you need. My power works best in weakness.' So now I am glad to boast about my weaknesses, so that the power of Christ can work through me. That's why I take pleasure in my weaknesses, and in the insults, hardships, persecutions, and troubles that I suffer for Christ. For when I am weak, then I am strong" (2 Cor. 12:9-10 NLT).

I've learned that I need to listen to God, as well as my body. My mind is generally willing, but my body isn't always able. I've learned how much I need to FROG it: Fully Rely On God—and that's a great thing! He's led me down a career path that allows me to utilize the skills He's gifted me, and it's something I never initially envisioned myself doing. But I love it, and I've never been happier.

Over the years, I've learned to adapt a bit, though it's still hard and frustrating to not always be able to physically do what I want to do when I want to do it. Thankfully, I'm blessed to have a very supportive husband, as well as a career that allows me to have the flexibility I need on a day-to-day basis. (And starting my editing career was something totally directed by God, too, but that's another story.)

I've found some hacks that seem to help me. Finding what works best for you is really only accomplished through trial and error. For me, regular massage and chiropractic appointments have been helpful, as well as the following things, in no particular order. Perhaps they'll help you, too.

SPEND TIME WITH GOD DAILY.
This is an important tip for anyone, whether they have a chronic illness or not. I have a devotional time daily, usually first thing in the morning. It helps me feel a bit more centered and prepared for what the day may bring. It also gives me a time to release some of the burdens I may be carrying by following this verse: "Don't worry

about anything; instead, pray about everything. Tell God what you need, and thank him for all he has done" (Phil. 4:6 NLT).

LISTEN TO MY BODY.
This is one of the most important items, and it is one that took me a long time to accept (along with the next item on my list).

KNOW WHEN TO ASK FOR HELP INSTEAD OF PUSHING THROUGH ON MY OWN.
This one is a challenging one for me, but I'm getting better at it.

UTILIZE TOOLS LIKE DRAGON NATURALLY SPEAKING.
This allows me to dictate and decrease some of my typing. While Dragon isn't perfect, fixing the errors is less stressful on my body than typing an entire manuscript or even emails.

PRACTICE MEDITATION.
This is a work in progress. I've seen benefits, but I'm not always great about making time in my schedule to do it.

LISTEN TO WORSHIP MUSIC.
This is one of the ways I feel closest to God. I often listen to worship music during my drive time each week. (Thank you, SiriusXM!)

TRY GENTLE EXERCISE (AS TOLERATED).
Exercise is important for everyone, even those with a chronic illness. However, the time and level definitely

varies. My tolerance level fluctuates throughout the week, or even the day, and I have different activities that I know work well for me. This will be yet another area of trial and error for each individual. Some things I've tried over the years are walking, Tai Chi, yoga, stretching, or programs designed for older adults or those with chronic illness (such as classes by the Arthritis Foundation or short Zumba Gold routines). I have learned how to make modifications that work for me, and some activities can even be done using a chair to reduce the stress on the body.

APPLY ICE AND HEAT.
Depending on my pain level and location, I use at least one of these on a near-daily basis. Some people, and some pains, respond better to one or the other. Your doctor may be able to help you determine which works best for your situation.

KEEP THINGS AT HEAD-TO-WAIST LEVEL.
I'm short, so this is a biggie for me. My husband is quite tall, but he's not always around, so I try to keep things I use regularly on shelves that are easily within my reach versus someplace that requires me to stretch beyond my comfort level.

PARTICIPATE IN SUPPORT GROUPS (MANY OF WHICH I HAVE FOUND ONLINE, SUCH AS THROUGH FACEBOOK).
I have found a number of groups for people dealing with similar issues. While no one there can offer me a fix or cure, it's nice to know I'm not alone, and that can be even more important on occasion.

EMPLOY FREQUENT BREAKS.

For years, I've been told that I need to take frequent breaks. However, it's not easy when I know I have work to do. I recently bought a sand timer (yep, old school!). It's purple (my favorite color), and it sits right beside my laptop where it's always in view. It's a thirty-minute timer. I occasionally go over, but in general, it really helps me to stay on a schedule of taking regular breaks, even if it's just to walk around for a few minutes.

KEEP WARM, BUT NOT TOO WARM.

My feet are always cold, and I found a heating pad designed for your feet. I love it! It has made me so much more comfortable throughout the day. I've also found that it's important to dress in layers. That way, I can adapt to every situation. When I get too cold, my muscles and joints feel stiff, so I try to combat this as much as I can.

I'm working on a book to share my story and encourage others to not give up because God hasn't given up on you. I may have chronic pain issues, but chronic pain doesn't have me. That can serve as a reminder for just about any situation you may encounter. And remember, you're not alone. God is with you. I've forgotten that on occasion, and I've found that He will place someone in my path to remind me that He hasn't left me and that I'm loved. I pray you come to the same realization. As the saying goes, "When you think you're at the end of your rope, tie a knot and hang on!" (I never liked hearing that, but I've learned that it's true.) God's not finished with me yet, and He's not finished with you, either.

I'd like to leave you with this reminder:

"This is my command—be strong and courageous! Do not be afraid or discouraged. For the LORD your God is with you wherever you go'" (Josh. 1:9 NLT).

Leslie is an author, editor, and reviewer. She's a member of American Christian Fiction Writers and The Christian PEN. Her devotionals have been published in compilations by Ellie Claire: Just Breathe, Refresh Your Soul, and Breathe: Devotions to Quiet the Soul. She has had flash fiction stories published, as well. Leslie is currently working on her first book, a devotional for women battling chronic pain and illness. In her spare time, Leslie enjoys reading, crocheting, spending time with family and friends (and her turtle!), and rooting for the NY Giants.

You can find out more about her on her website: www.lmckeeediting.wix.com/lmckeeediting. You can also find her on her blog lmckeeediting.blogspot.com, on Twitter @lmckeeediting, and on Instagram @lmckeeediting.

CARRIE DEL PIZZO

I'VE HAD HEADACHES ALL MY LIFE. As a kid, my head would hurt if I didn't eat for a few hours, but an apple usually fixed the problem. In my twenties, the migraines started. One headache a month was easily managed with Excedrin and a good night's sleep. Pregnancy migraines were a little tougher. The pain was far more severe than anything I had ever experienced. I'm talking about knock-down, drag-out, throw up, and crawl back to bed kind of pain. And I couldn't take anything with aspirin. At one point, my doctor gave me narcotics for the pain, along with anti-nausea meds usually used by chemotherapy patients. The heavyweight prescriptions seemed extreme to me, but it was enough to get me through the relatively short term of pregnancy. I knew there would be an end date, so I just had to wait it out.

By the time my youngest child was two years old, my headaches had made a fairly significant leap. My head hurt every day, all afternoon, into the evening. While a single Excedrin had been enough to eradicate a headache in the past, now I was taking two and three pills a day, sometimes with little effect. Fiery pain engulfed the entire left side of my head and frequently woke me in the dead of night. Of course, I couldn't sleep through that level of pain and ended up tossing and turning for several hours each night. And the lack of sleep naturally translated to another headache the following day.

With three energetic little ones depending on me, napping wasn't an option. Mom doesn't get to be sick. And it never occurred to me to go to the doctor. It's just a headache. Right?

Early in the summer of 2008, I woke up one morning at 5:30 a.m. Not intentionally, of course. (I'm a morning person, but I'm not crazy.) But there I was, bright-eyed and bushy-tailed for no apparent reason. I decide to make use of my time in the quiet before my kids woke up and shuffled downstairs to hang out with Jesus. What a sweet time I spent in the Word and prayer! If only my devotional times could be so rich every morning.

Well, guess what. The next morning, I mysteriously woke up at 5:30 again. By the third or fourth day, I finally took God's hint and agreed to rise at 5:30 each morning to spend time with Him. No alarm needed. My brain just woke up. I was able to read His Word without the kids interrupting. I sat quietly and listened for His voice. I wrote pages and pages in my prayer journal. Never had I so enjoyed my time with the Lord.

And then came Friday, July 25, 2008. As usual, I read Scripture (don't even remember what passage) before turning to Oswald Chambers' *My Utmost for His Highest*. My particular copy ends each day's devotional with a brief prayer. On that day, this was the prayer: "Lord, of late I feel a dim uncertainty as if Thou are leading me into a domain of truth that as yet I have not entered or penetrated. Lord, lift me up till I see Thee; hold me until I fulfill Thy purpose."[3]

Looking back, it seems like a normal enough thing for a Christian to say. Lead me; I want to see You; hold me; and so forth. But in that moment, these words pierced my heart. I knew without question that God

---

[3] Oswald Chambers, *My Utmost for His Highest: the Golden Book of Oswald Chambers: Features the Author's Daily Prayers*, Grand Rapids, MI: Discovery House, 1994.

was speaking directly to me. The only "dim uncertainty" was where He was leading me. But the facts I knew without question were that He was leading; I was going to understand a new truth about Him; and He would hold me until the end. I heard His voice clearly tell me that whatever was coming would be big; it would be difficult, it would take a long time, and He would be holding me every step of the way.

As a strong Christian who has walked with Christ and maintains a sturdy faith in my mighty God, my first response was just like virgin Mary when the Angel of the Lord told her she would give birth to the Son of God. "May it be done to me according to your word" (Luke 1:38 NASB).

Wrong! I was terrified. My thoughts immediately turned to all the terrible things that could happen to my family. I imagined bleak diagnoses, tragic accidents, and evil crimes sure to leave physical and emotional scars. I cried, begged, and bargained with God—even while I knew I needed to surrender. I tried to cut a deal: I'd live through whatever He sent my way as long as He didn't touch my husband or children—well, just don't let them suffer—okay, just don't let them die. After six months of fruitless negotiations, I finally gave in.

"Lord, I trust You."

Late in February 2009, on a Friday evening at ten, my husband drove me to the ER. I'd had terrible abdominal pains for three days and had finally had enough. At four in the morning, I donated my appendix to science and went home thirty-six hours later. A couple weeks of recovery and I was back to chasing the kids around, washing piles of laundry, and cleaning a house that never seemed to get clean.

Wow! That wasn't so bad. I don't know what I had been so worried about, but God really did take care of me on that. And the experience wasn't nearly as bad as I had feared. Piece of cake. Easy peasy. No biggie.

But you and I both know, if it seems too good to be true, it is.

About a month after my appendectomy, I started having passing moments of slight dizziness. Then I had days of fatigue. After a few weeks, I started walking funny; my legs seemed to have a mind of their own. As though I was wearing swim fins, I picked my knees up high and flopped my feet back down. My family started calling me Flipper. (Don't worry. I laughed right along with them.)

In the weeks that followed, the slight dizziness felt like being on the high seas in a hurricane. The fatigue became an inability to lift my head from the pillow. And the flipper walk started to look like a severe cerebral palsy.

My personal medical philosophy has always been, "If I ignore it long enough, it will go away," and that philosophy had served me well for many years. Add to that the fact that a good night's sleep reset my legs to a normal walk. On top of it all, my headaches had suddenly stopped. All of these things together meant I waited about two months before going to the doctor, until my family finally badgered me into it.

In the space of about six weeks, I saw the nurse practitioner, my family doctor, an ear/nose/throat specialist, a chiropractor, a neurologist specializing in multiple sclerosis, and a physical therapist. I had blood tests, x-rays, an MRI, a CT scan, water in my ears, lights in my eyes, exercises for fixing, and exercises for coping. Nothing worked—mostly because no one could figure out what was going on.

Eventually, God landed me in the office of a neurologist who specializes in headaches. I wasn't having many headaches in those days, but he didn't like the tales of my bad days. And so began the trial and error method of finding a low dose blood pressure medication to control my migraines. I have naturally low blood pressure, but the doctor explained the low dose was just enough to keep my brain level. And we were both pleasantly surprised to find that adjustments to the migraine medication also had a positive effect on my fatigue and funny walk.

Over the last decade, my condition has grown and developed and changed. I've learned a lot about my health, though not much about my brain. The thing is, doctors don't really know much about the brain. My neurologist once thought he would eventually wave a small device over a patient Star Trek-style, see what was wrong, and prescribe a simple medication. Now he says that the more he learns about the brain, the less he knows.

So, a decade later, he still doesn't know exactly what's going on with me, but we've pinned down a few details. The funny walk with severe fatigue is called Episodic Ataxia. Basically, every muscle in my body falls asleep instantly while my brain is still awake. Just like when I'm asleep, my heart rate slows; my breathing steadies; and I can't move my body. Generally, I can feel it coming, notify my family or friends, and get myself to bed—quick! It's particularly embarrassing when it happens at work or at church because I have to be carried to the car. Humiliating. Only once has it happened while I was driving. I made it home, but the experience was terrifying. If it ever happens again, I will immediately pull over and call for help.

But here's the really great news: God has been with me every step of the way. When I was referred to a Multiple Sclerosis specialist, I had peace. When I'm too tired to join my family in bocce ball or swimming, I find great pleasure in watching them. When I can't make my body move, I have a super comfy bed for sleeping.

Don't be fooled into thinking I'm some sort of super Christian who has an irritatingly happy attitude about everything. Far from it. It's very frustrating that I can't carry a half full glass across the kitchen without spilling it. It's embarrassing having to ask strangers to open doors or pick up things I can't reach. I grow weary of the expressions of pity from friends and strangers alike. I definitely have days when I'm so tired I want to cry. And I do.

But on those really rough days, God sends someone along to show me His love and care. Usually my husband or mom is close enough to slide a shoulder under my tears and ask the Lord to sustain me. My kids have always been happy to retrieve a water glass or open a door for me, but now that they're teenagers, they've begun to step in with emotional support as well.

By seeing Mom suffer and watching Dad and Grandma hold her up, my children have learned to pray for others. I don't mean saying, "Oh, I'll be praying for you," the way we all say it and then forget it. No, I mean actually stopping what they are doing to pray for me right there on the spot when I'm having a tough day. And I've seen them do it for others as well. Friends, I have to tell you, that makes it all worth it for me.

And I've learned something as well. I had read so many times how the apostles had praised God while they were in prison and the earthquake shook the prison doors open. Surely, they knew this would happen, and that's why they praised Him. Nope. They were just praising Him because He's God.

Does this sound crazy to you? It sure sounded crazy to me. How can you praise God when there's nothing to praise Him for? When, in fact, there's actually quite a lot to complain about?

I've had some time to rethink my attitude on praise. When you're lying in bed unable to move, you have plenty of time to think stuff through. And here's what I came up with. I don't praise God because of my health and strength. I thank Him for those things, the same way I thank Him for His provision and blessing and gifts. But that's not what praise is about.

Instead, I praise Him because He's God.

I praise Him because He's holy.

I praise Him because He's worthy.

Whether I'm feeling strong or weak, rich or poor, happy or unhappy, He's still God. And that's why I praise Him.

Yes, it's been a long, hard road. No, I don't know when I'll be healed. Maybe I won't be. But that doesn't change the fact that He is God and He is worthy of my praise.

These days, I work from home. I had to quit my regular day job because I couldn't keep up. As a freelance editor, my stress level is way down, and my bed is ten feet from my desk, just in case. My standard prayer is for enough work to pay the bills, and I've made it a habit to thank God for His faithful provision.

Living with migraine and episodic ataxia is a management lifestyle filled with regularity. Regular diet, regular sleep, regular schedule. Nothing ever changes, and my body likes it that way. Best of all, my God never changes, and my body is thankful for that, too.

In this world of texts, memes, and emojis, slowing down to truly communicate can feel like straining a muscle you haven't exercised in far too long. Seventeen years of business experience across a variety of industries has taught Carrie Del Pizzo the fine art of professional communications. Partnering with corporate executives and entry level employees alike, she has written and edited major project proposals, marketing handouts, sensitive client communications, employee handbooks, and user manuals.

Carrie's love of literature and story have led her to develop and exercise her fiction writing skills. Aside from her personal creative efforts, she also edits for self- and traditionally-published authors and enjoys writing short dramas for church presentation.

Whether you're writing a novel or a short story, a career-making proposal or a blog post, Carrie can help you get your message across clearly and concisely, and help you use your most effective words every time.

Visit her at www.carriedelpizzo.com.

TOM DONNAN
LIVING TIME BOMB

LIVING IN THE DASH. I FIRST heard this from a pastor who was riding the elevator with me. Short ride, powerful thought. He said it is how we live in the dash from the date of birth to the date of death that ends up on our tombstones. It is the living in the dash that is important. In retrospect, I have had a very good life. Filled with challenges, struggles, and burdens. Life!

Twice in my life, I have been suicidal. The first time was at age fourteen. My mother died two years before, and my dad became a mean machine. I did everything I could to stay out of his way. That worked for only so long. His pain management was to vent on me. Ouch! My older sisters had families; my closest sister was off elsewhere; and I was and felt alone. If you could believe this, it could have been worse, except for my niece who was three years younger than me. She would give him a piece of her mind on how badly he was treating me and, shockingly, she reached him. He would relent for a time. Finally, at fourteen, the thought of ending it all entered my mind. The spiritual and physical pain was terrible. The bridge over these troubled waters was an invitation to join Sea Scouts at my church. This ended my thoughts of ending it all.

Moving the dash forward sixteen years, I was now married, had two children, and worked at a very good job. However, the struggles continued. It wasn't until later I would learn about generational cycles, spiritual and physical. But for now, I was thirty, and my favorite sister was dying of cancer. She had colon cancer and had moved into her final days. It hit me right where my pain is concerning the death of my mother, who died of breast cancer at the age of fifty. Now my sister, Sandy, would not live to see her fortieth birthday. However, things were not the same as before.

In the late seventies and early eighties, there was a fantastic move of the Holy Spirit. Sheila, the sister who took care of me when I was a baby while my mother was having terrible migraines, was swept up in God's grace and accepted His gift of salvation. Her life was drastically transformed, and she shared her newfound relationship with God with her family. She was annoying. I pushed her away; don't talk about Jesus to me. Other siblings did hear the Good News she was sharing. I was the last holdout—a tough nut, resistant to change and stuck in the cycle of never-ending pain.

Sandy was spending the last days of her life at Rush St. Luke's hospital near downtown Chicago. I was determined not to be excluded from hospital visits like when my mom was near her end. I drove down to the hospital, arriving just before eight in the evening, and settled in. I stayed with Sandy all night in the recliner until it was time to go to work. Every other day, this was my routine. I noticed a strange occurrence during this time. The hospital staff were coming in to see her and spend time in her room. The presence of God was so sweet, they wanted to be with her to be refreshed in His loving atmosphere. Then it happened.

As usual, we were watching TV; and out of the blue, she turned to me and said, "Tommy, if you invite Jesus into your heart and life, He will help you with all of your problems." Then she turned back to watch TV. But something happened to me. I couldn't let it go. Although I was exhausted keeping this routine, I couldn't sleep, tossing and turning thinking about making a decision. Should I accept or reject her challenge to me? She was my sister, two weeks from her death, telling me in a selfless manner that Jesus could help me. The weight of life was killing me. I needed help and a change.

On May 7, 1983, at 6:30 p.m., I invited Jesus to come into my heart and life. It was as if I had lived in a cave all of my life. I had been in the dark, and here came Jesus, entering my dark existence with Light. Truly, for the first time, I could see (spiritually). To say my life changed is an understatement. I had no idea of the plans God had for me. I entered a supernatural life by experiencing Him.

I have been having God dreams and visions, experiences and visitations ever since. He has led my life in powerful ways. In this journey, He has showed me what is coming ahead. I have looked to see the fulfillment of the dreams. I have learned the ways of God over the last thirty-six years of following Him. That is how I knew I would be okay.

A hereditary cycle in my family is coronary heart disease. I had no fear; I knew I was going to survive. I had seen things in my future and knew this was the end of life for me. I was only forty-seven years old. Now I had three heart stents, and heart muscle damage was limiting life. My normal was gone. Life with medication began. So many pills. I was at the mercy of those who have the education; and in my vulnerability, I now trusted. It didn't go well. The side effects of the medication were horrible. I went back and forth between my two doctors. They would say that my physical problems were not in response to the medication they prescribed. Back and forth I went. My bowels would work only once a week. I ran a low-grade fever; the aches were horrendous. So, I stopped all medications, figuring it was better to live life feeling somewhat like what I had before. I figured it took forty-seven years to clog my veins the first time, and it would take another forty-seven to do it again. Wrong!

My spiritual life had been off the charts. Really, I could not get a pastor to help me understand my God experiences. They were so beyond the norm of our day; I had no way of knowing God was preparing me for an America that will need the renewed power of God to survive. So, I grew in spiritual maturity as I moved toward the end of my life.

In March of 2001, I was experiencing a heavy spiritual burden for the Chicago Metro area. When it came upon me, I was compelled to pray that God would protect my city. Day after day, this heartfelt burden came upon my heart as I interceded in prayer, not knowing why. The burden ended on September 11, 2001. I don't know why, and it brings up all kinds of questions concerning New York. Even though Chicago was an alternative target, no planes attacked the city.

Again, I was having a burden not to pray but to be aware. For six months, I felt a message in my spirit. It was, "Don't wait; take actions immediately." Then it came. February 6, 2006, I was working out at the gym when the chest pain began. It was a level five on the pain scale. I ended my routine and went home to talk with my wife. Sitting in the computer/office bedroom I asked her to call the fire department. Boom, my vein closed.

Do you ever question God? I do. Like, Lord how did I end up living in this house? It is a three minute drive from the fire station. It is six degrees out, and there is now six inches of snow on the ground and still snowing. The call was made, and I thought it would be easier for the paramedics to work on me in the kitchen. I got up, walked to the first of three steps down into the kitchen, and collapsed back into the hallway. The doorbell rang, and they rushed in, placing baby aspirins and nitro pills in my mouth. They cut off my shirt to get the IVs in my arms.

On the stretcher, out the door, snow fell on my chest before they pushed me into the ambulance. The police had also showed up and had shoveled the driveway for the stretcher to get through easily. It was cold. I was in the most pain of my life. Two morphine shots did not stop the pain. We headed to the hospital, and I began to look for the light. You know, the light people say they see as they are dying? Odd what happens at times like these. I knew I had not even begun to finish what God had shown me that was ahead of my life. But within my emotional heart comes the knowing that I have lived a really good life. I felt peace with it. I was fifty-four years old. My children were grown and had really good lives. As we were alongside the golf course en route, I told the paramedics I felt a rolling fire beginning in my toes and rolling up my legs. They told me not to worry about it. Those were the lasts words I heard.

One of my Bible heroes is the apostle Paul. When he talked about the rapture, he tells us it will happen in the twinkling of an eye. Or in other words, it will be so fast, we do not perceive motion as we move from one state to another. That is how it happened for me. One moment, I was in the ambulance, and the other I was in the afterlife. My heart stopped, and instantly I was in the spiritual realm. I had no fear; I know I am God's and will be with Him after life. Right then, I was looking at the peaceful golf course, and I was in no pain. Looking around in fascination, I heard the voice of God. He said to me, "It is only while you are on Earth that you can work for Jesus." His voice. It is deep and masculine and rolled across the landscape, leaving a lasting impression. Bam!

Unknown to me at the moment, someone was yelling, "Clear!" I have no idea how many times they shocked me with the defibrillator; as before, it happened so fast, there was no mental observation to motion. A man leaned over, talking into my left ear, saying, "Tom, all your stats look good." I was at a loss to know why he was telling me until three days later, while in ICU, a doctor came in and asked me how it felt to be back from the dead. That is when all the pieces came together. I had had the widow-maker heart attack. Only three percent of those who have this heart attack live to see another day. My fourth stent was now in place.

For six months, when I saw an ambulance on TV, I would go into a panic attack. This experience was traumatizing. We live life thinking we have time ahead to do as we plan in the daydreams of our days. Nope. Not always true. This changed my life. I got busy, first of all, dedicating to God in a full, emotional heart press. However, now I had a new normal from the other new normal from my first heart attack. Now I had limited heart function, and my life was limited. The best was yet to come.

I had prayed for physical healing of my heart from the first day of the first heart attack. God had given me what I would call small healings. Now, in my mind, I needed a big one. He had not answered my cry before because He knew I would have two.

About six months after the second attack, I was taking a nap on a Sunday at around three o'clock in the afternoon. This was when I was young enough to rest my head on my inner arm, where I listened to the one beat of my heart—pump. Then, I heard a loud, roaring wind that was nearly deafening. It first started high above me and came closer. I did not feel any manifestation of the Holy Spirit. Yet as I lay there, I heard pump, pump. Yes, I was hearing two beats of my heart. I have MRIs showing heart damage and MRIs showing no heart damage. My heart doctor took me off most of the meds, saying I no longer needed them. Praise God!

I returned to normal life. It has now been twelve years since I died. When I talk in churches, I tell people I was not a keeper; God threw me back. I praise God He did because I love doing His work. I must take two pills a day—a baby aspirin and cholesterol meds to keep my veins open. Everything in life I want to do, my body will do for me. Praise God!

I traveled with a friend who has a revival healing ministry, and I have seen hundreds instantly healed and delivered. I have had twelve more years to love my children and grandchildren. I have written five books in my hopes of aiding people to have a relationship with Father God. In short, I love doing the work for Jesus. Although I live with the ache that comes with the meds and struggle when life hits my tender spots, I live to touch people's lives another day.

For ten years, I have been an online minster for Need Him Ministries, an evangelistic site where I can log in and chat about Jesus with anyone who comes in from anywhere in the world. I have had thousands of one-on-one conversations about the Christian life and God's plan of salvation. In John 3:1-8 (NIV), it says:

> *Now there was a Pharisee, a man named Nicodemus who was a member of the Jewish ruling council. He came to Jesus at night and said, "Rabbi, we know that you are a teacher who has come from God. For no one could perform the signs you are doing if God were not with him." Jesus replied, "Very truly I tell you, no one can see the kingdom of God unless they are born again." "How can someone be born when they are old?" Nicodemus asked. "Surely they cannot enter a second time into their mother's womb to be born!" Jesus answered, "Very truly I tell you, no one can enter the kingdom of God unless they are born of water and the Spirit. Flesh gives birth to flesh, but the Spirit gives birth to spirit. You should not be surprised at my saying, "You must be born again." The wind blows wherever it pleases. You hear its sound, but you cannot tell where it come from or where it is going. So it is with everyone born of the Spirit."*

I have come to believe this is the meaning of life. It is how we find our way into a relationship with Father God and receive the gift of His spiritual birth through Jesus Christ. If you want this gift, please pray:

Dear Father God,

I thank You for Your Son, Jesus, and the work He did on the cross, shedding His blood to pay for the sins of all mankind. I tell You, Father, I am a sinner. I am sorry for the pain my sins have caused You. Please forgive me. Now, Lord,

I invite Jesus to come into my heart and life, and I want to live for You. In Jesus' Name I pray. Amen.

Tom Donnan is the author of Healing the Nation, Spiritual House Cleaning, Pastors and the Presence of God, 7:14 Angels on Assignment, and One Door Between Us.

Visit him on Amazon at www.amazon.com/Tom-Donnan or on Facebook at Healing the Nation Ministries: www.facebook.com/HealingTheNationMinistries. You cans send him an email at healingthenation1776@gmail.com.

RENEE BLARE

MY NAME IS RENEE BLARE, AND I'm a CRPS Warrior. I'll explain what CRPS is in a minute, but first, how about I tell you how I developed this little-known disease?

I had my "routine" right knee replacement in May of 2017. Pain is to be expected with surgery; but in my case, the pain only grew exponentially over time instead of receding and going away. Nothing stopped it; nothing made it better. Nothing made it bearable. I couldn't walk. I couldn't sleep. I couldn't breathe. It took over a year before one doctor (after eleven others) put a name to what was happening to me—Complex Regional Pain Syndrome, Type 2 or Causalgia.

Victory? No, relief. I no longer felt like I was insane. This pain wasn't in my head (as several doctors had told me.) I wasn't "faking it" as friends and family accused me and, truth be known, still do. Of course, now that I think about it, how do you "fake" drop foot, abnormal EMGs (electromyography), and bipedal temperature changes of three to four degrees? I guess I must have control over my body more than any person alive! (Yes, that's sarcasm. I apologize. I'm a tad bitter. God's working on me.)

Since being diagnosed with CRPS, my life has changed. I've been around the grief cycle twenty times at least. I can no longer drive a car short or long distances. I've lost my twenty-plus-year career as a pharmacist and pharmacist manager. My disabled, but loyal, husband, whom I previously cared for in many ways, is now my caregiver. Physically, I walk with a staff, take high doses of opioids in order to tolerate intolerable pain levels, and need regular adjustments to my spinal cord stimulator. My body is broken in multiple areas, and I nor anyone else can fix it.

You'd think I'd join the thousands who have taken their lives because of my excruciating pain and hopeless future, wouldn't you? After all, it isn't called the "Suicide Disease" for nothing. I'm not going to say I haven't thought about it. Any irrational human being in intolerable agony has. But I have something that always keeps me from the final step—hope.

Each day, I turn to the one Person Who offers me eternal relief and hope and another who has experienced chronic pain longer than me—Jesus Christ and my husband, James.

The future isn't hopeless. I may wake up to pain every morning, but I have joy. I know one day when I open my eyes, I'll see the glory of Jesus. Until then, I find my husband next to me. This godly man is a grumpy bear in the morning, but he'll do anything to take a sliver of my pain.

If you suffer from CRPS, fibromyalgia, MS, or any debilitating disease, you don't need to walk alone. You may not have the love of a husband, family member, or friend, but you can have the unconditional love of God. Jesus suffered the most painful death imaginable on the cross—for you! Don't believe me? Read about it in the Bible! These eyewitness accounts have been validated and are admissible in court. Discover what Jesus went through for YOU! Research what a Roman scourging and crucifixion entailed. God went through this for you so that He could say He has walked in your shoes. He paid the ultimate price for you. Why would He, God, in the flesh, do that? So that YOU can spend an eternity with HIM in Heaven, NOT Hell.

You will probably tell me you live in hell already. Oh, no, you do not. What if the pain you experience every day was multiplied by one hundred, two hundred, one thousand? What if you never slept? Never, ever found reprieve or a moment's rest? That, my friend, is HELL.

CRPS Type 2 is as close to Hell as any on this Earth. I don't want to experience the real thing, and above all, I do not want it for you. Jesus died for you and everything you've done to separate you from Him. And He's done all the work for reconciliation!

How do you get to Heaven? Believe it or not, you don't have to "do" anything, except believe in Jesus as your Lord and Savior. How do you do that? Confess that Jesus is God and walked on this Earth as man, died on the cross for you, and rose from the dead three days later. Believe that He died for the things you've done, do, and will do in this life to separate you from Him (sin is what the Bible calls them) and build a relationship with Him, so you can learn His ways that won't separate you from Him in this life.

He wants to bear the burden of your pain, giving you the strength to make it through the days ahead. If you've managed pain this long without Him, can you imagine what you can do with Him? Think of all the decisions you've made so far! This one should be rather easy, don't you agree? He's waiting, and I can't wait to hear your answer!

You can read more about Renee Blare on her blog, www.crpshuntforfreedom.wordpress.com, and you can go to Amazon.com to learn more about her books: Beast of Stratton, To Soar on Eagle's Wings, Crazy Woman Christmas, Through Raging Waters, and Racing Hearts.

RESOURCES

I AM LISTING A FEW PLACES where more information can be gained for those who suffer from chronic conditions, such as fibromyalgia, autoimmune diseases, IBS, IC, migraines, CRPD/CRPS, etc.

While this isn't an exhaustive list, it is a beginning. The more you learn about your condition(s), the better you are able to adjust. I know by experience. I continually return to certain websites, learning more, reading about updates, refreshing my knowledge, and looking for advice or answers.

Living with a chronic condition is on-going, and every tidbit of knowledge helps us become victors instead of victims.

AMERICAN ACADEMY OF PAIN MANAGEMENT:
www.painmed.org

AMERICAN PAIN SOCIETY:
www.ampainsoc.org

ARTHRITIS FOUNDATION:
www.arthritis.org

FIBROMYALGIA NETWORK:
www.fmnetnews.com

FIBROTOGETHER:
www.FibroTogether.com

National Fibromyalgia Association:
www.fmaware.org

National Headache Foundation:
www.headaches.org

Health Central Migraine:
www.HealthCentral.com/migraine

HealthRising, Finding Answers for ME/CFS and FM:
www.healthrising.org

Mayo Clinic:
www.mayoclinic.org

National Fibromyalgia Research Association:
www.fmaware.org

U.S. Pain Foundation:
www.uspainfoundation.org

American Academy of Pain Medicine:
www.painmed.org

American College of Rheumatology:
www.rheumatology.org

American Chronic Pain Association:
www.theacpa.org

BOOKS FOR ADDITIONAL READING

The Arthritis Experts at Mayo Clinic. *Mayo Clinic on Arthritis.*

Bartz, Brooke. *Chronic Love: Trusting God While Suffering with a Chronic Illness.*

Good, Phyllis Pellman. *Fix-it and Forget-it Cookbook.*

Jacqueline, Ilana. *Surviving and Thriving with an Invisible Chronic Illness: How to Stay Sane and Live One Step Ahead of Your Symptoms.*

Johnson, Elizabeth A. *Touching the Hem: A Biblical Response to Physical Suffering.*

Lewis, C.S. *The Problem of Pain.*

Mayo Clinic. *Mayo Clinic Guide to Pain Relief, Second Edition*

For more information about
Daphne Self
and
Journey On
please connect at:

www.authordaphneself.blogspot.com
www.facebook.com/authordaphneself
@AuthorDaphneS
www.instagram.com/authordaphneself
www.goodreads.com/authordaphneself
www.bookbub.com/authors/daphne-self

For more information about
AMBASSADOR INTERNATIONAL
please connect at:

www.ambassador-international.com
@AmbassadorIntl
www.facebook.com/AmbassadorIntl

Thank you for reading, and please consider leaving us a review on Amazon, Goodreads, or our websites.

More from Ambassador International

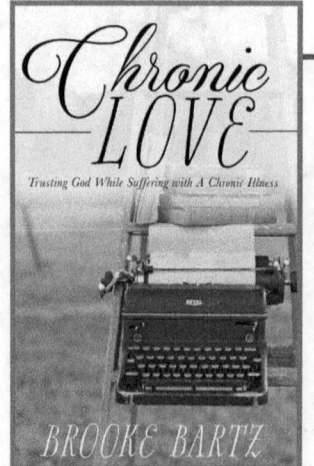

In *Chronic Love*, Brooke Bartz reveals a deeply raw and descriptive account of life with a chronic and debilitating illness, and she shares with readers how comfort and strength can be found through the Truth in God's Word.

Specifically designed for women who daily battle chronic illness, *Chronic Love*'s goal is to provide solid Scriptural encouragement for the fight.

Moms living with a chronic illness face a unique set of challenges and can often feel isolated. *Yet Will I Praise Him* uses God's Word to help moms understand why they have a chronic illness and how it can help them grow in faith by exploring a host of difficult questions. Hannah uses her own struggles to share biblical hope and practical advice.

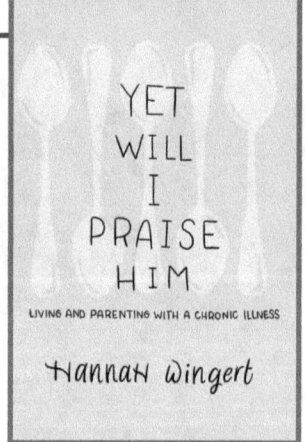

Dr. Jim Halla, a practicing rheumatologist and a National Association of Nouthetic Counselors fellow, knows from experience how to use the Scripture to help those suffering pain. In his medical practice, Dr. Halla regularly treats and counsels hurting patients.

In *Pain: The Plight of Fallen Man* Dr. Halla shares his wisdom with those who hurt and those who are trying to help.

www.ingramcontent.com/pod-product-compliance
Lightning Source LLC
LaVergne TN
LVHW051523070426
835507LV00023B/3271